The definitive guide to the rise & fall of

BRITISH
STEAM

igloobooks

igloobooks

Published in 2013
by Igloo Books Ltd
Cottage Farm
Sywell
NN6 0BJ
www.igloobooks.com

SHE001 0813
2 4 6 8 10 9 7 5 3 1
ISBN 978-1-78197-384-4

Written by Claire Welch and Dr Jonathan Little

Printed and manufactured in China

The definitive guide to the rise & fall of

BRITISH STEAM

Contents

Interactive instructions

On your mobile, or tablet device, download the **FREE** Layar App.

Look out for the **SCAN WITH LAYAR** logo and scan the whole page.

Unlock, discover and enjoy the enhanced content.

Available on the iPhone
App Store

Google play

SCAN WITH
layar
See page 5
for instructions

layar

For more details, visit: **www.igloobooks.com**

Introduction

It could never have been predicted in the early 19th Century that, over 200 years later, British steam trains would ultimately come to be viewed with so much affection and nostalgia.

Steam engines were not originally intended to carry passengers, but freight; railways were at first derided as blots on the landscape, and in no way regarded as the scenic wonders they later became - integral to, and enlivening, the British countryside (with all their accompanying architectural splendors - in the form of picturesque and imposing branch and mainline stations, and hundreds of innovative, cleverly-designed bridges, tunnels and viaducts).

Indeed, the very concept of these fearsome mechanical monsters scything their way through the unspoiled British countryside, carrying fire in their bellies and relentlessly belching out smoke and steam, was certainly regarded with abhorrence by the great 19th Century landowners - until the day finally arrived when these same landowners not only came to admire the thrilling sight of a passing steam train, but to demand their own local, or even private, railway station.

Main: Steam travel experienced a revival in the second half of the 20th Century as enthusiasts began rescuing locomotives and rolling stock and setting about preserving the heritage. This modern version of the Orient Express is still extremely popular in the 21st Century.

Main: A drawing from the Illustrated London News depicting steam launches and a diver's barge searching for bodies and survivors of the Tay Bridge disaster in Dundee. Seventy five passengers died when their train was plunged into the Tay as the bridge collapsed underneath them in stormy weather on New Year's Eve 1879.

Furthermore, early steam engines, carriages and rolling stock, were very far from safe – the rough ride they often provided was occasionally terminated by such major disasters as derailments (often due to cracked rails), rock falls, all-too-frequent boiler explosions, tunnel crashes, and sometimes even bridge collapses – most notably culminating in the confidence-shattering Tay Bridge disaster of 1879, resulting in the loss of an entire train and of the lives of all 75 souls believed to have been aboard. But after every such tragedy, important lessons were learned, and safety and engineering improved.

Above: A man balances on the edge of the Tay Bridge to view the disaster scene.

*Above: Scottish engineer James Watt (1736-1819) was an inventor who was
at the forefront of the development of steam engines – a vital driving force
of the Industrial Revolution. In 1774, together with his business partner
Matthew Boulton (1728-1809), he established a factory manufacturing
steam engines in Soho, near Birmingham, of which this is a view.*

By a process of the most relentless technical innovation,
and through constant improvement and evolution – with
numerous patents relating to steam engines (and indeed
railways in general) being applied for each year from the
late 1700s onwards – every aspect of Britain's sophisticated
railway system was to lead the world technologically
for much of the 19th Century, and well into the 20th.
Thanks to a cycle of continuous economic investment
(often speculative), British railways did much to drive
the increasingly frenetic pace of life and industry – both
fuelled by, and fuelling, the boundless entrepreneurial
spirit of the age – such that British steam ultimately
became a crucial factor in the development of businesses
both great and small, and indeed in all the other complex
regional and national enterprises that helped to build and
maintain the largest and most sophisticated commercial
trading empire that the world had yet seen.

Main: The Industrial Revolution that saw a transition to new manufacturing processes began in Britain around 1760 and within a few decades had spread to Western Europe and the United States.

Telling its extraordinary story through the aid of a rich array of historic illustrations, each section of this book deals with a unique aspect of the development of British steam. An overview of the history of the steam engine, and insights into its practical workings, helps to establish the context for the unfolding of the far-reaching story of the rise of British steam railways, their golden age, and ultimate demise. Along the way, we recall the genius of British invention, and the grand vision of those far-sighted pioneering engineers, who continued to emerge in unending succession from the early days of the Industrial Revolution. Individuals such as Thomas Newcomen (1664-1729), Matthew Boulton (1728-1809), James Watt (1736-1819), Richard Trevithick (1771-1833), George Stephenson (1781-1848) – the "Father of the Railways" (working together with his son, Robert) – Isambard Kingdom Brunel (1806-59), and on into the 20th Century, with Sir Nigel Gresley (1876-1941). Less obvious are the contributions of many others, whose crowded lives, marked by astonishing achievements, precipitated a cascade of rapid technological advancements that continue to reverberate down to the present day.

Above: Two innovators whose vision provided the impetus for the development of the steam railways: Isambard Kingdom Brunel (right) – one of the best known engineers of the 19th Century responsible for building the Great Western Railway – and Robert Stephenson (seated on the left), designer of the pioneering steam locomotive 'Rocket'.

Main: Isambard Kingdom Brunel's Elizabethan hammer beam roof and colonnade at the Great Western Railway Station at Temple Meads in Bristol circa 1845.

Main: Britain's network of canals was well established by the end of the 18th Century. Here, a horse drawn barge moves across the Bridgewater Canal Aqueduct at Barton, near Manchester, in 1793 while a river barge passes beneath. This aqueduct, built by James Brindley in 1765, was moved when it was replaced in 1896, and can still be seen in Barton.

TO ENGINEERS AND IRON FOUNDERS.

THE DIRECTORS of the LIVERPOOL and MAN-CHESTER RAILWAY hereby offer a Premium of £500 (over and above the cost price) for a LOCOMOTIVE ENGINE, which shall be a decided improvement on any hitherto constructed, subject to certain stipulations and conditions, a copy of which may be had at the Railway Office, or will be forwarded, as may be directed, on application for the same, if by letter, post paid.

HENRY BOOTH, Treasurer.

Railway Office, Liverpool, April 25, 1829.

Above: This advertisement was placed in the "Liverpool Mercury" newspaper on 1 May 1829 by the Liverpool & Manchester Railway for an improved locomotive engine.

Nᵒ 2.

LIVERPOOL, OCTOBER 5, 1829.

A LIST OF THE ENGINES

Entered to contend at RAINHILL, on the 6th of OCTOBER instant,

FOR

THE PREMIUM OF £500,

OFFERED BY

The Directors of the Liverpool and Manchester Rail-road,

FOR THE

BEST LOCOMOTIVE POWER.

No. 1.—Messrs. Braithwaite and Erickson, of London; "The Novelty;" Copper and Blue; weight 2T. 15CWT.

2.—Mr. Ackworth, of Darlington; "The Sans Pareil;" Green, Yellow, and Black; weight 4T. 8CWT. 2Q.

3.—Mr. Robert Stephenson, Newcastle-upon-Tyne; "The Rocket;" Yellow and Black, White Chimney; weight 4T. 3CWT.

4.—Mr. Brandreth, of Liverpool; "The Cycloped;" weight ; worked by a Horse.

5.—Mr. Burstall, Edinburgh; "The Perseverance;" Red Wheels; weight 2T. 17CWT.

The Engines to be ready at Ten o'Clock on Tuesday Morning. The Running Ground will be on the Manchester side of the Rainhill Bridge.

The Load attached to each Engine will be three times the weight of the Engine.

No Person, except the Directors and Engineers will be permitted to enter or cross the Rail-road.

J. U. RASTRICK, Esq., Stourbridge, C.E.
NICHOLAS WOOD, Esq., Killingworth, C.E. } Judges.
JOHN KENNEDY, Esq.; Manchester,

Above: Page 37 from the notebook belonging to one of the judges, John Urpeth Rastrick (1780-1856), used to record details of the Rainhill locomotive trials in 1829. The Rainhill Trials were a competition set up to find the most efficient locomotive for railway haulage on the Liverpool & Manchester Railway. The competition was won by the 'Rocket' designed by Robert Stephenson (1803-1859) and George Stephenson (1781-1848).

It was the seminal Rainhill steam engine trials of 1829 that may be said to have firmly ushered in this entrepreneurial and optimistic new age, in which the general pace of life was to quicken rapidly – and continue to quicken – right up to our own times. Goods, people and information were all set on a path of faster and further travel and distribution.

Already past its prime was Britain's nationwide canal network – the first, yet slow, means of mass conveyance – which relied on horse-drawn barges, and which had seen its monopoly on goods transportation peak around 50 years earlier, during the first, or initial phase of the Industrial Revolution. The rise of steam locomotion coincided with, and was indeed partly responsible for, the second great phase of the Industrial Revolution – the start of which roughly coincides with the date that Queen Victoria came to the throne, in 1837. Yet even by that time, there already existed some of the main arteries that still today underpin Britain's rail network. The remarkably enterprising Victorian age will forever be associated with the rise of British steam – not only as a means of rail travel, but because steam engines were ultimately to power boats, ships, factories, agriculture, earthworks and much else besides.

The end of what some historians define as the Second Industrial Revolution (circa 1870) neatly coincides with the era in which steam railways began to be firmly established, reaching new heights of technological refinement. It was also the time when the "iron road" began to turn into a true steel railway – largely thanks to Sir Harry Bessemer's invention of a furnace that could turn wrought iron into steel in sufficiently large quantities to allow for the mass manufacture of steel that was so badly needed to provide truly sturdy, unbreakable rails, for heavier and faster trains.

The splendid Edwardian age – the period immediately prior to the Great War – saw rail passenger numbers rise to an all-time peak: to such a level indeed, that similar numbers of travellers would not be seen again on Britain's railways until the present day, 100 years later (and bearing in mind that today the nation's population is one third larger than it was then). The Edwardian age was also the peak of Empire – when Britain held sway over 400 million subjects – and this period saw steam trains and rail technology being exported globally, often as part of a strategy to help control and maintain the Empire and its trade.

Main. The Prince and Princess of Wales watch the Bessemer steel process at the Cyclops Works in Sheffield in August 1875. Sir Henry Bessemer (1813-1898) learned metallurgy working in his father's foundry. In 1856, in response to demand for stronger cannon able to fire a new type of artillery shell in the Crimean War, he invented the Bessemer process, enabling molten pig-iron to be turned into steel by blowing air through it in a tilting converter. This was the first process for producing large amounts of good quality steel cheaply, originally to produce guns, but later to supply tracks to the growing railway industry.

Steam-driven railways were, of course, bound to supersede canal traffic, as they could carry a great deal more freight, were cheaper and much faster. Rail companies even bought out some ailing canal companies and laid lines where once water flowed. The opening of the Stockton to Darlington line in 1825 demonstrated the possibilities of this new means of freight transportation. Trains could also speed up postal deliveries, and by the 1840s and 1850s they came to absorb much of the work of official Mail Coach Services.

While rail companies had envisaged that there may possibly be some desire for passenger travel in addition to freight haulage on the early networks, it was ultimately passengers themselves that demanded services be made available for their use, and to an extent that was quite unforeseen – since steam trains had evolved first and foremost as the Leviathan servants of 19th-Century British heavy industry.

London's hugely popular and eye-opening 1851 Great Exhibition of the "Works of Industry of all Nations" (effectively an enormous showcase for the arts and manufacturers of the British Empire) – was an important catalyst in encouraging unprecedented numbers of visitors to travel by train, many doing so for the first time. There were six million visitors to the Exhibition during 1851, which roughly equated to one third of the entire population of Great Britain at that time. With 13,000 exhibits from around the globe, the world was truly coming together, interconnecting, and its people were on the move.

Above: The South Eastern Railway Company's express train 'Folkstone' designed by T R Crampton on display at the 1851 Great Exhibition in the Crystal Palace, London.

Main: A train at a station about to depart with a Louth to London mail coach at the rear of the train. The expansion of the railway network led to the demise of the horse-drawn Royal Mail coach in the 1840s.

Main: A railway cutting, possibly on the Great Western Railway line between Bath, Somerset, and Bristol. Isambard Kingdom Brunel was appointed chief engineer of the GWR in March 1833, with the task of building a railway to link London and Bristol. The first section, opened in 1838, went from London to Taplow, Buckinghamshire, and the line finally reached Bristol in 1841. The GWR was the first to install an electric telegraph alongside its lines.

Above: Avon Wharf was home to one of the Midland Railway's goods depots in Bristol. Goods were brought into this depot by ship, or by rail to be shipped abroad. By the end of the 19th Century, Bristol docks had seen a major increase in traffic.

While Joseph Paxton was busy designing the innovative Crystal Palace in which to house the Great Exhibition, other larger-than-life engineers like Isambard Kingdom Brunel were fast becoming the real "movers and shakers" of the age – being one of a select group of visionary individuals who viewed steam locomotion as part of a much wider picture of worldwide industrial development, enabling the transportation of people and the facilitation of trade well beyond British ports.

The great port of Bristol, for example, at the terminus of the Great Western Railway (founded in 1833), was to be the embarkation point for travel onwards by steamship, all the way to the New World, and even the Southern hemisphere – thus as far as it was possible to roam. Through providing such opportunities for travel, steam technology engendered not only a social revolution, but a psychological revolution, too: the upper, middle and eventually working classes could all literally expand their horizons; they could speed up and broaden their personal business transactions and their communications.

This inevitably began to lead to the changing of perspectives, and even beliefs. Above all else, the process of developing the steam engine seemed a living embodiment of a concept that chimed so well with the tenets of the great industrial era. The "Protestant work ethic" found its perfect rationale in the diligent work of engineers such as George Stephenson, whose example was so praised by Victorian "self-help" advocate, Samuel Smiles: through invention, refinement, and unceasing toil, nature could be tamed, mysteries understood, and life could be altered and improved.

The famous 'Puffing Billy' was an engine that set new standards of mechanical reliability as far back as 1813-14, although by later measures, many such early engines were slow, and prone to accident or breakdown (the rails being as much a problem as the engines). There were so many unknowns and worries in the early days of steam, even as the engines themselves improved: could any man or woman actually travel at 60 miles per hour (or faster), and not suffer permanent damage to their health? Such fears, of course, soon proved to be unfounded, and engines continued to become faster and much more reliable from the mid 19th Century onwards.

By the latter part of the century, these steam-driven marvels were affording passengers the ability to travel great distances in carriages of extraordinary luxury and craftsmanship – especially those First Class carriages manufactured by the British Pullman Car Company. Much had changed since passengers had initially climbed aboard steam trains, although rail companies long operated on a three-tier class system. Third class was at first no more than a rough ride in an open wagon, but even for this lowest class, standards improved – especially where companies competed for passengers – and so travel became reasonably comfortable for all classes by 1900.

Above: The perils of travelling Third Class! As the passengers try to shelter under their umbrellas one man's is blown inside out, causing him to lose his top hat to the wind.

Main: 'Puffing Billy' was built by William Hedley (1779-1843) in 1813, for use at Wylam Colliery near Newcastle. Hedley was an English inventor who proved that loads could be moved by the traction of smooth wheels on rails. The locomotive was finally taken out of service on the conversion of Wylam Railway from five foot to a narrower gauge and was then acquired by the Science Museum in London.

Main: *Chancellor of the Exchequer William Gladstone (front row, near right) with directors and engineers of the Metropolitan Railway Company on an inspection tour of the world's first underground line, 24th May 1862. Built between Paddington and the City of London, it opened in January of the following year.*

Above: The middle of the 19th Century saw railway companies adopt Greenwich Mean Time to standardize timetables. Here a notice informs the British public of a change in time as clocks go back an hour in the daylight saving scheme that was first introduced during the First World War.

Even allowing for the fact that there needed to be so much investment in rail infrastructure, passenger train travel was relatively cheap throughout much of the 19th Century. Gladstone's Railway Act of 1844 enshrined the right to affordable travel on at least one designated train per day, on every route, stopping at every station – and with adequate seating and at least some protection from the weather. This Railway Act was in many ways a tacit recognition of the early existence of a burgeoning "commuter" class – people who wished to use the train to travel daily to work, or in search of work. The railway enabled people to seek employment where their particular skills were most needed. Capitalism was certainly transforming life and working practices, but also providing some opportunities for personal change, and flexibility, in the process.

So much new and unexpected came with the railway. The railway timetable was just one innovation we take for granted today, but its effect was far-reaching. The urgent, practical need for consistent timetabling precipitated the standardization of clocks, first in cities along the main route of Brunel's Great Western Railway (where "railway time" was introduced in 1840). This concept soon became more widespread, until by 1848 almost all rail companies came to adopt Greenwich Mean Time as their common standard. It can therefore be argued that 19th Century railways, in conjunction with steam-powered factory mass production methods, did much to create our modern Western notion of time – and of our attitudes to how periods of work and of leisure are best divided up and categorized.

Above: Box Tunnel was one of Isambard Kingdom Brunel's major engineering achievements on the Paddington to Bristol line. Construction began in 1838 and it was opened to traffic on 30 June 1841. It is on a continuous gradient of 1 in 100 falling towards Bristol and its total length is 1 mile and 1452 yards (2,939 metres).

With the aid of railways, newspaper distribution increased enormously, and books were sold in stations (indirectly advancing literacy), while all sorts of fresh exotic produce and perishable goods began to appear, far from their original source of production. Rail also aided a boom in the construction industry, by transporting the necessary building materials even to fairly remote areas (since there was little that couldn't be carried by rail); and, of course, the very construction of the railways, and the lessons learned in their building, were to revolutionise civil engineering throughout the world. While necessity drove continual invention, it should not be forgotten that much toil and suffering lay behind the construction of newly-completed marvels such as the nearly two-mile-long Box Tunnel (opened in 1841) and the wondrously picturesque Settle to Carlisle Line (opened in 1875). These extraordinary feats of engineering were achieved at the cost of the lives of many of the rugged, labouring navvies – or railway "navigators" – this term betraying its origins in the days when the pioneering canal system was being dug, in the period immediately preceding the laying of the railways.

Main: A steam locomotive emerges from Box Tunnel. The long tunnel dug through Box Hill, Wiltshire, between Bath and Chippenham was the longest railway tunnel in the world when it was completed in 1841. The lives of about 100 navvies were lost during the course of its construction, which took five years and cost six and a half million pounds. The rising sun is said to shine straight through the tunnel every year on 9 April, Brunel's birthday.

Main: In 1808, Richard Trevithick established a "steam circus" in Euston Square in London, charging members of the public one shilling for the opportunity of riding on a carriage pulled by his locomotive, the 'Catch Me Who Can'. It was built at the Hazledine foundry at Bridgnorth, Shropshire, and weighed eight tons. The ride, which was capable of travelling at speeds of up to 12 mph, was popular with the London public, but the weight of the locomotive broke the rails, and it closed after two months.

Much progress had been made since Richard Trevithick commenced his steam locomotive experiments in the latter years of the 18th Century. Trevithick first showed how the great stationary machines of the past could be transformed into steam locomotives when he ran an engine in Merthyr Tydfil in 1804 that travelled nine miles while pulling over ten tons, though at a maximum speed of only five miles per hour. In 1808, Trevithick next tantalized the public and potential investors in London with his "steam circus" – intended to demonstrate the steam engine's superiority over horse-drawn travel – by erecting a circular railway on which ran a new engine named 'Catch Me Who Can' (reaching 12 miles per hour). But in the very early 19th Century, steam locomotion was still regarded by many as no more than a curiosity.

Such visionary experiments continued to gain momentum in the decades to come, leading inexorably to the production of the most famous and memorable locomotives of the 20th Century: the 'Flying Scotsman' – recorded in 1934 as being the first steam locomotive to reach 100 mph; and then 'Mallard' in 1938 reaching an official 126 mph – the fastest speed ever recorded for a steam-driven locomotive. And for the public, as much as for the numerous rail workers of the day, such trains, complete with all their carriages and vans, and looking resplendent in their colorful individual company liveries, were not only huge sources of national pride, not only extraordinary masterpieces of intricate engineering – they were sleek and beautiful. But, as ever in the history of technology, just at the moment of steam locomotion's greatest triumph, it was becoming increasingly clear that new forms of propulsion would, within a very few decades, come to supersede steam power. The railways were running into economic difficulties, too.

Above: Steam locomotives had certainly changed since the days of Trevithick's steam circus. The A4 Pacific class 'Mallard' was designed by Sir Nigel Gresley, the chief engineer of the London & North Eastern Railway (LNER). On Sunday 3 July 1938, the 4-6-2 locomotive reached a speed of 126 mph (203 kph).

TRANSPORT ACT 1947

GREAT WESTERN RAILWAY COMPANY

LONDON MIDLAND & SCOTTISH RAILWAY COMPANY

LONDON & NORTH EASTERN RAILWAY COMPANY

SOUTHERN RAILWAY COMPANY

LONDON PASSENGER TRANSPORT BOARD

Notice is hereby given that in pursuance of the above Act the Undertakings of the above named bodies vest in the British Transport Commission on 1st January, 1948, and that on and after the said date all Byelaws, Regulations and Notices published by any of the said bodies and in operation immediately before the said date and all tickets, consignment notes and other documents issued or used on and after the said date and which bear the name of any of the said bodies shall be deemed to be published and issued by and in the name of the Railway Executive or the London Transport Executive (as the case may be) constituted under the said Act.

BY ORDER

31st December, 1947

Above: The 1947 Transport Act was the Act of Parliament under which the Labour Government nationalized Britain's railways. The Act came into force on 1 January 1948 and amalgamated the Great Western, London, Midland & Scottish, London & North Eastern and Southern Railway companies, together with the London Passenger Transport Board under the control of the British Transport Commission.

During the Great War, Britain's railways were brought under government control, just as they were in the Second World War. But it was after this First World War that the creeping symptoms of under investment began to appear, at the same time that passenger numbers began a long and steady fall throughout the coming decades – in the face of increasing competition from buses, lorries, and all other forms of motorized transport. The 1948 Nationalization of the "Big Four" rail companies (GWR, LMS, LNER, and SR) – already consolidated in 1923 – was a last opportunity to undertake long-overdue upgrading and reforms, and to put railway economics onto a sounder footing. (Nationalization had previously been advocated at various times throughout the 19th and early 20th Centuries, but never before acted upon.)

Despite various well-intentioned (though sometimes misguided) efforts, even the 1955 Modernisation Plan did not prove a success. And despite early problems, the increasing viability of less labour-intensive diesel and electric locomotive propulsion systems was to sound the death-knell of steam locomotion. Finally, the uncompromising, perhaps even ruthless 1963 report of the first Chairman of British Railways, Dr Richard Beeching, entitled "The Reshaping of British Railways", seemed clearly to mark steam's last rites. Steam officially died on 11th August 1968, along with a good deal of the former infrastructure that had sustained it.

Main: A worker applies a transfer of the new British Railways logo to the side of a locomotive to mark the nationalization of the railway industry.

Main: The National Railway Museum was established in 1975 and boasts a collection of over 100 locomotives and nearly 200 other items of rolling stock. This replica of the Liverpool & Manchester Railway (L&MR) 0-2-2 'Rocket' (Replica) was built in 1979.

As steam locomotives, mighty and small, lay rusting in sidings and scrap yards in the late 1960s, dedicated individuals and preservation societies were able to buy and commence restoring some, and a selection were already being preserved for the public in what is now the National Railway Museum in York. (As far back as 1862, London's Science Museum had the foresight to acquire Stephenson's influential 'Rocket' – the design winner of the 1829 Rainhill trials – and several of the larger rail companies themselves did much to preserve their most notable locomotives.)

But even if we are to leave aside for a moment the whole notion of the romance of British steam – however impressive it was, and however much it was once a cause of enormous pride and satisfaction (such that many still regard the steam era with a gnawing sense of loss) – there is yet another reason why we should, necessarily, continue to commemorate the heroic age in which our railways were born: for in the end, the steam engine not only moved Britain, it ultimately moved the world; and, in so doing, it did much to create the foundations of our modern way of life.

Above: Derelict locomotives at Barry, South Wales, in 1977. After steam locomotives were withdrawn from British Railways in 1968 some were preserved, but most were scrapped. The scrap yard on Barry Island was run by Woodham Brothers and around 100 locomotives were scrapped here. The site concentrated on scrapping rolling stock first so many locomotives were left here until the 1980s. However, around 200 locomotives were rescued from the scrapyard and preserved.

A History of the Steam Engine

It is a testament to the genius of British invention and design that continually-improved versions of the steam locomotive became the staple of rail transport throughout the world for almost one and a half centuries; and a variety of steam engines still continue in operation today - not just on "heritage" lines, but doing the real work for which they were originally intended: hauling freight and carrying passengers, according to a pattern first established in the early years of the 19th Century.

Henry Grote Lewin wrote in his important 1914 account of the early development of "The British Railway System" that to ascertain who exactly was "the originator of our railways is a difficult if not impossible task". That same difficulty is multiplied when it comes to determining who first had greatest insight into harnessing the full potential of steam pressure to create an engine of real practical use.

Main: Steam locomotives changed the way freight was hauled.

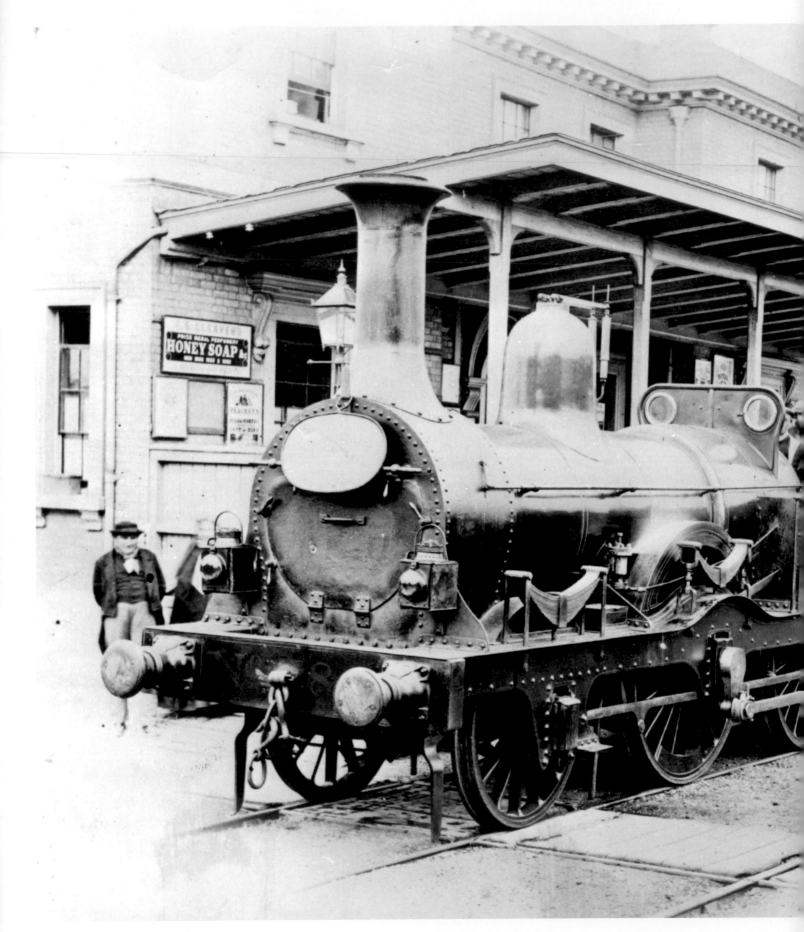

*Main: This steam locomotive of circa 1870 is a far cry
from the first inventions and demonstrates the technological
advances developed during the Victorian era (1837-1901).*

But while Lewin found it surprising that no-one before the early 20th Century seemed to have compiled a summary of the earliest development and evolution of the railway system, by contrast, right from the start of the 19th Century, there were writers who felt it important to document not only the past history of the steam engine, but also contemporary developments in that field. There was a clear sense that the steam engine was not only something radically new, but a technology that was capable of revolutionizing life. Steam engines later came to be acknowledged as the most influential breakthrough in human technology throughout the entire span of the Victorian period. And most interest in early 19th-Century studies on steam was focused on innovations permitting steam's application not so much to the great powerful stationary engines first developed in the 18th Century, but to motive power – or 'locomotion'.

The 1821 Act of Parliament authorizing the building of the Stockton & Darlington Railway introduced a relatively new concept (one that was still then gaining currency): that of 'loco-motive or movable engines'. Before this date, the term 'steam engine' would merely have tended to suggest a stationary steam engine. A new word was needed to distinguish stationary from mobile or self-propelling engines. Indeed, so novel was the term 'loco-motive' (deriving from the Latin, the broad meaning of which is "pertaining to movement from a place") that many parliamentarians and officials of the time did not fully appreciate what this term really meant. When, for its 1825 opening, George and Robert Stephenson built an engine specifically for the Stockton & Darlington Railway – the world's first (publicly subscribed) passenger-carrying line – it was named 'Locomotion No 1'. This engine is calculated to have hauled as many as 700 people on its inaugural journey, to the utter astonishment of the huge crowds of onlookers.

Above: Thomas Savery, one of the early steam power innovators.

One early and important book on the history of the steam engine was published at a time of crucial locomotive developments. Entitled "Historical and Descriptive Anecdotes of Steam-Engines, and of their Inventors and Improvers", its author was civil engineer Robert Stuart. In his book, published in 1829, Stuart surveyed a vast array of many kinds of steam engine over a period of 2,000 years, from the era just before the birth of Christ, right up to contemporary developments. He impressed on his public the leaps forward made by Thomas Savery, and in particular those of Thomas Newcomen, before devoting much time to James Watt's multifarious experiments. Stuart later concentrated on recent "rotary" (or "rotative") steam engines (where a piston drives a flywheel, as distinct from a stationary rocking "beam" engine – developed in order to help pump water out of mines). Beam engines (without a flywheel) represent the first large-scale practical application of steam, while those later beam engines connected to a flywheel, enabling rotary motion, owed their existence to the necessity of finding a power source for all types of factory machinery. Stuart even featured early illustrations of experiments with true "rotary" engines – being, in effect, crude forms of steam turbines. He showed just how many steam oddities were created through the ages, before finally summarizing progress by including a valuable chronological list of steam-related patents, from 1630 to 1828.

One other highly significant contribution to the growing number of treatises of how steam engines developed, and how they work, appeared in 1852. Likewise covering the "History of the Steam Engine, from the Second Century Before the Christian Era to the Time of the Great Exhibition" (in 1851), this book, by Robert Wallace, avoided the detailed technicalities of earlier writers on the subject, and set out instead to "supply the want of a cheap and popular History of the Steam-engine" – there being by the mid-19th Century a huge new interest in these mechanical marvels amongst the general populace. Wallace stressed the thoroughness of his research nonetheless, and his reliance on "authentic sources" – having consulted the writings not only of previous historians but of the actual inventors of the technology, including "the original specifications and notes of James Watt himself". Wallace's praise of steam knew no bounds: it was like some new deity or genie that possessed an ability to transform all the fundamentals of life through its seemingly magical properties. In the Preface to his popular history, Wallace lauds "the amazing and exhaustless resources of Steam Power, exemplified in the progress of national and international communication among all the enlightened countries of the world."

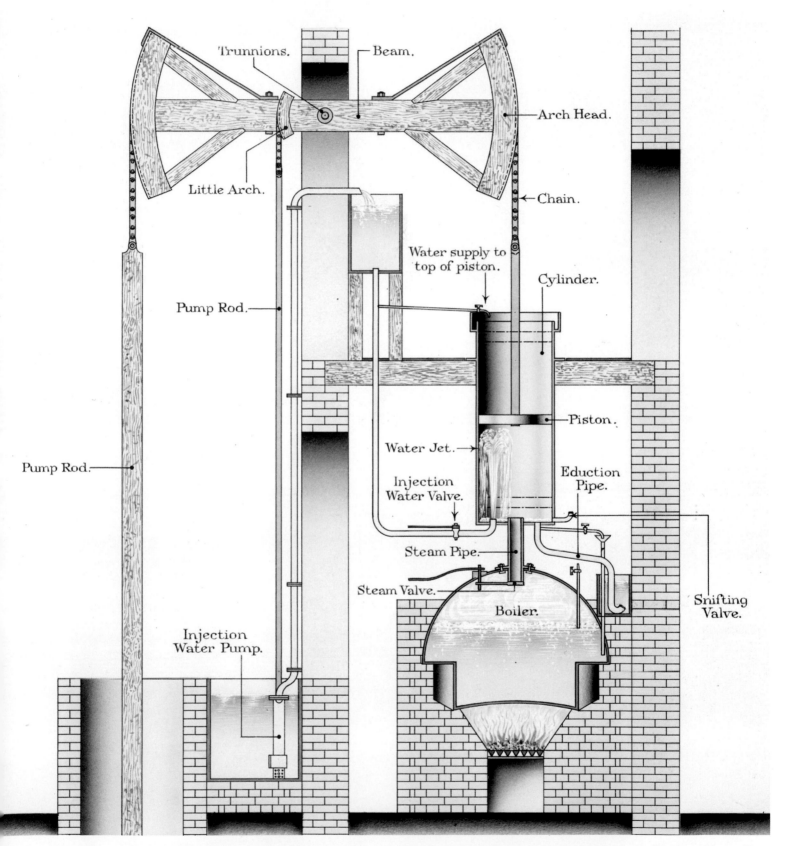

Trunnions.

Beam.

Arch Head.

Little Arch.

Chain.

Water supply to top of piston.

Cylinder.

Pump Rod.

Piston.

Water Jet.

Education Pipe.

Injection Water Valve.

Pump Rod.

Steam Pipe.

Snifting Valve.

Steam Valve.

Boiler.

Injection Water Pump.

Main: A sectional drawing of Thomas Newcomen's 1712 pumping engine.

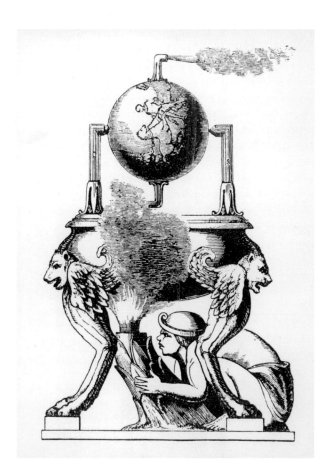

*Opposite: Greek mathematician and
engineer Hero (or Heron) of Alexandria,
with the help of a naked young man,
conducts an experiment that later evolved
into this aeolipile steam engine (above).*

Most such writings on the development of the steam
engine commence with the crucial experiments of Hero (or
Heron) – an ancient mathematician, geometer, mechanic,
and expert in 'pneumatics' (through which knowledge
he created devices operated by air, steam or water
pressure). Hero is thought to have taught at the Museum
in the great and learned metropolis of Greek-founded
Alexandria, in Ancient Egypt, and supposedly flourished
in the early decades of the 1st Century. From his own
writings, we learn of his 'steam kettle' that had the force
to lift a ball into the air, and his quite spectacular steam-
driven 'reaction machine' (or reaction steam-turbine,
also known as an 'aeolipile' – which literally means 'wind
ball'). This 'aeolipile' was effectively the world's first
rotary engine, working on the rocket principle. It caused
a ball to rotate on an axle when steam was fed into it, the
steam then being exhausted through short bent nozzles
on either side of the ball – so generating rotating motion.
Hero's numerous other inventions included pumps, a host
of ingenious automata, a 'water organ' and a complex,
dragon-shaped 'steam oracle' for temple use – where,
by means of steam pressure, a great beast was made to
speak supernaturally (these oracular utterances then
being interpreted by priests)! This particular religious
oddity is in fact extremely important because it anticipates
Thomas Savery's demonstration of the raising of water by
steam pressure by over one and a half millennia. And it is
more than possible that there existed rudimentary steam-
powered devices – about which we no longer have any firm
evidence – even earlier than those documented by Hero
of Alexandria. Previous writers from the ancient world
make obscure references to what could be steam engines,
including the Roman architect Vitruvius, who also wrote of
aeolipiles in his famous treatise, 'De Architectura', in the
1st Century BCE.

Hero's aeolipile is not known to have had any practical use (that is, it was not seemingly harnessed to anything), though it would certainly have been helpful in demonstrating to students the 'laws of nature'. It was the 1550s before the Ottoman inventor and polymath Taqi al-Din (1526-85) was to describe another such steam turbine, but this time a steam-powered machine that did have real mechanical use: it turned a roasting spit. Other related devices that worked on the steam turbine principle – known as 'steam jacks' – were also described by Giovanni Branca in Italy in 1629, and in England by John Wilkins in his 'Mathematical Magick' of 1648. These devices were again used for automatically turning a spit (although heat from smoke, or mechanical weights, could also be used for this purpose).

Leaving aside various extraordinary Renaissance-era proposals as to how steam could best be harnessed – not the least of which was Leonardo da Vinci's steam-powered, iron-ball firing, artillery piece (inspired by the inventions of Archimedes) – Denis Papin in France (1647-circa 1712) must next be mentioned for both his theorizing and practical experimental exploration of the possibilities of steam for use in pumping, and propulsion. Papin importantly proposed that rotary motion could be obtained from a reciprocating action, by utilizing two or three steam cylinders with pistons ascending and descending that could drive into and withdraw from pinions on a rack, linked to a paddle wheel shaft. Papin's work is also notable for his realization of the importance of the safety valve – without which boilers would explode above a given pressure, if such a valve was not present that could manually (and later automatically) release excess pressure.

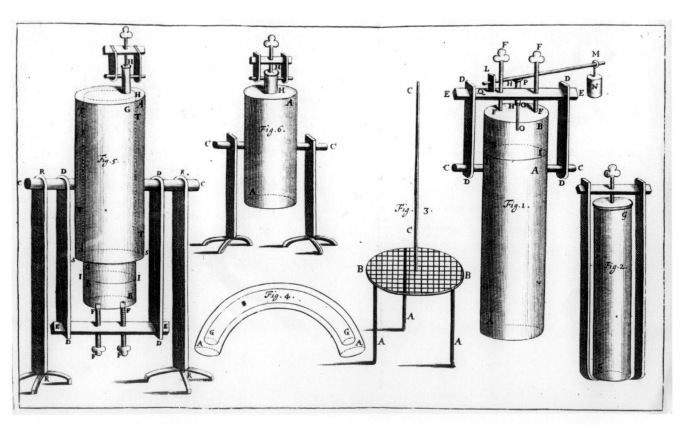

Above: Diagram showing French physicist Denis Papin's steam-digester, or pressure-cooker, for softening bones for soup.

Main: French scientist and inventor Denis Papin.

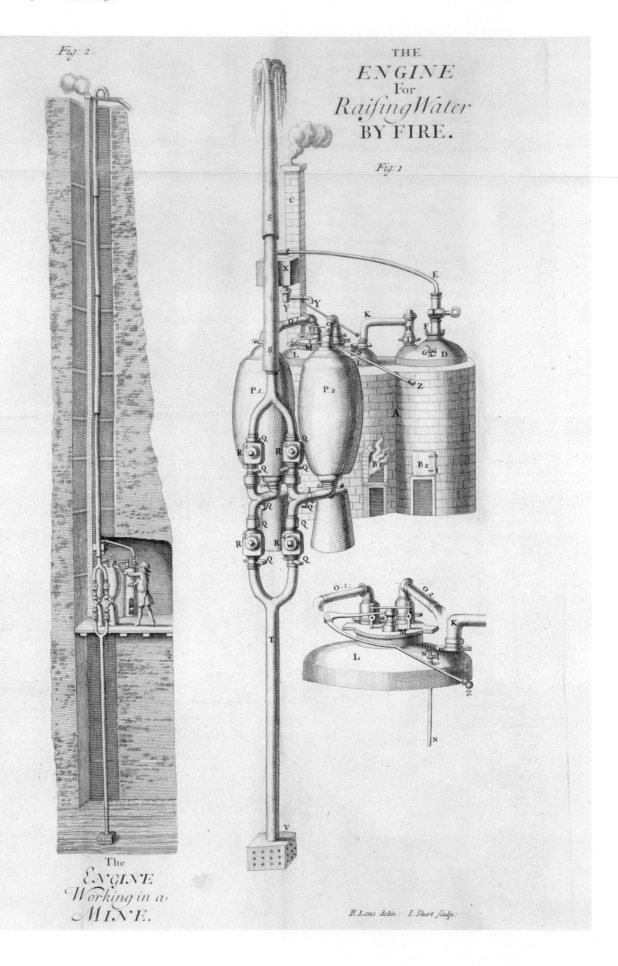

Fig: 2.

THE
ENGINE
For
Raifing Water
BY FIRE.

Fig: 1.

The
ENGINE
Working in a
MINE.

B. Lens delin: I. Sturt sculp:

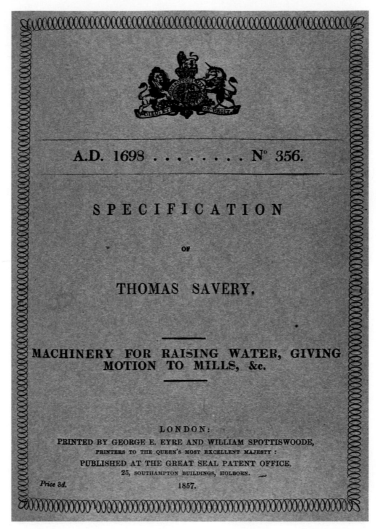

Above: The title page of the Savery patent (No 356) for a pumping steam engine.

*Opposite: Illustration of Savery's early steam pump from 'The Miner's Friend'
or an 'Engine to Raise Water by Fire'.*

Papin's theoretical models evolved from his work on the 'steam digester' (a sort of pressure cooker), a subject on which he spoke to the Royal Society in London in 1679. Papin is remembered today as laying the foundations for the first modern steam engines because in 1690, having previously worked alongside the great physicist and chemist Robert Boyle, Papin built a model piston-driven steam engine – believed to be the first in the world – and went on to describe an 'atmospheric steam engine'.

English military engineer and part-time inventor Captain Thomas Savery (circa 1650-1715) contributes to the story of steam power through his patenting of the first crude steam engine, which he called a "new invention for raising of water and occasioning motion to all sorts of mill work". He exhibited a model of his apparatus before the Royal Society in 1699, right on the verge of the new century that was to witness the first Industrial Revolution. But Savery's engine – a sort of thermic siphon – had no piston or moving parts apart from its taps, and was generally inefficient. Savery's subsequent 1702 public engine demonstrations in London were said to produce steam "eight or ten times stronger than common air" – or as we now say, at a pressure of 8 to 10 atmospheres. But repeatedly, the early years of the 18th Century saw Savery's boilers and mechanical construction methods prove insufficiently strong for the forces demanded of them, with joints breaking, and pressures becoming so great that in one mine pumping experiment of around 1705, the steam pressure "rent the whole machine to pieces".

Above: The steam engine invented by Thomas Newcomen in 1712 consisted of a pump designed to reduce water in the galleries of mines.

Drawing on the ideas of both Savery and Papin, iron monger Thomas Newcomen (circa 1664-1729) introduced a revolutionary atmospheric engine in 1712 – the year that Denis Papin is thought to have died a pauper. This was, at last, the world's first truly practical steam engine, and it was used for pumping water out of deep mines. At first, Thomas Savery's "Fire Engine Act" patent of 1798 effectively forced Newcomen to enter into partnership with Savery, since Savery's was an all-embracing patent in relation to any "engines that raised water by fire". Newcomen's steam engine design was novel in that it incorporated a piston. The vacuum created when the steam was condensed drew down a piston that was used to work a beam engine, which rocked on a central fulcrum. Brass piston cylinders were much later replaced by massive iron ones up to six feet in diameter, once the Coalbrookdale Company in Shropshire had pioneered new and better iron casting techniques from the 1720s to the 1760s. Newcomen's engine worked purely by atmospheric pressure, so avoiding the dangers of using Savery's high-pressure steam – a technical argument that was to be echoed later between Richard Trevithick (who advocated high-pressure steam, with all its dangers) and James Watt (who favoured low-pressure steam). Very early steam locomotives – including those built by Trevithick, and in particular Hedley's 'Puffing Billy' of 1813-14 – show their clear evolution from piston-driven beam engines. When applied to the first locomotive engines, the beam rocked not a free-moving fly wheel, but directly powered a drive wheel placed firmly on an iron track. Gears were tried as a means of transferring power to the wheels, notably in Trevithick's first true steam engine conceived in 1803 for the Ironworks at Pen-y-darren in South Wales, but gearing (and even chain drive) were ultimately abandoned in favour of using more efficient piston-driven crankshafts linked to piston rods by connecting rods, with coupling rods joining the wheels. (Coupling rods first appeared on the Stephenson-built 'Locomotion No 1'.)

Main: Piston and rod from Newcomen Pumping Engine 'Old Sarah', Newmarket Silkstone Colliery, Stanery, near Wakefield, Yorkshire.

Main: The haystack boiler at Farme Colliery, Rutherglen, which was made in the 1730s and was one of the first to use Thomas Newcomen's steam engine.

Main: Scottish engineer and inventor James Watt as a young boy sitting at a dining room table with his parents while experimenting with steam released from the tea kettle.

*Right: Matthew Boulton formed a partnership with
James Watt in 1773 to produce steam engines.*

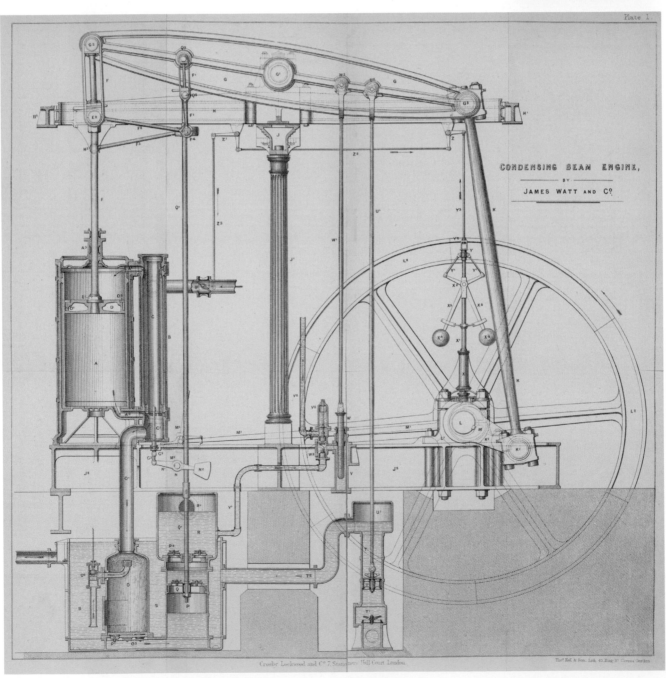

Plate I.

CONDENSING BEAM ENGINE,
BY
JAMES WATT AND C°.

*Above: A condensing beam engine by
James Watt & Co, late 18th Century.*

*Above: James Watt as a young man
with his early steam engine.*

There used to be a schoolchild's riddle and aide memoire: "What [Watt] was the name of the man who invented the steam engine?" This was not so much a question as a statement, but it is not technically correct, for while Scottish mechanical engineer James Watt (1736-1819) did not invent the steam engine, he had such an eye for detail and made so many improvements to Newcomen's engine, that it could now become the true driving force behind Britain's Industrial Revolution. Watt and his business partner, Matthew Boulton (1728-1809), were granted a monopoly on the building of steam engines with a separate 'condenser' – a vital leap forward – though many tried to circumvent their monopoly in order to innovate. Watt's condenser ensured that the main cylinder never lost heat. Ten years of effort also saw Watt finally develop accurately-bored cylinders for his engines, so that little steam was wasted – this innovation in turn being made possible by John Wilkinson's invention in 1774 of a high-precision cylinder-boring machine. Two years later, in 1776, Boulton and Watt built their first commercial engine, and by 1783 Watt had developed a 'double acting' reciprocating steam engine capable of turning a flywheel with great regularity. Watt's patents finally expired in 1800 – at which time he retired from business. It was also Watt who developed the concept of 'horsepower' as a way of measuring power or engine performance, by averaging the work that could be carried out by a mine pony.

Part of the impetus for experimenting with steam power in the early 19th Century had been born of the necessity of finding cheaper means of transportation than horse power – as horse fodder had become much more expensive in the aftermath of the Napoleonic Wars (which we also have to thank in 1799 for the introduction of income tax). Conversely, improvements in mining were making the coke that powered steam engines more plentiful, and consequently cheaper. The earliest clear instance of such economic stimulus driving improvements in motive steam power is shown by developments at the Middleton Colliery outside Leeds. When increasing feed prices, coupled with a shortage of horses, threatened the viability of the entire colliery business (rapidly rising costs quickly making transportation of coal prohibitively expensive), John Blenkinsop (1738-1831) began in 1808 to design, and within five years patent, a rack-and-pinion steam traction engine. His machines were later claimed to be "the world's first commercially successful steam locomotives". Matthew Murray (1765-1826) and his company built the engines for Blenkinsop, with the rails being made at the Hunslet Foundry. The two locomotives that went into regular service on 12 August 1812 – 'Salamanca' and 'Prince Regent' – hauled six and eight wagons, each containing three and a quarter tons of coal (as stated in a "Leeds Mercury" report about the first trial run, on 24 June). It is worth noting that George Stephenson's initial locomotive design owed much to Murray's engine: Stephenson was deeply impressed when he first saw the new engine on a visit to the colliery in 1813. As a result of quicker and better distribution methods, Middleton Colliery was able to produce a record 100,000 tons of coal by 1814 – a fact not lost on colliery and factory owners. Indeed, the world of manufacturing and commerce as a whole took note of such outstanding industrial success resulting from the use of steam technology.

Left: Collieries all around the country saw the benefits steam locomotives could bring. This is the 'Springwell Colliery Engine No 2', County Durham.

Just as with Stephenson's enormous triumph at the
opening of the Stockton & Darlington Railway 13 years
later, thousands of spectators came to cheer on Murray
and Blenkinsop's unusual new train in 1812. The "Leeds
Mercury" stated that their engine trial was "crowned with
complete success" – realizing at once its applicability "to
all railroads". The invention was also recognized as being
"of vast public utility". And, where previously there was
a desperate concern how to obtain more "equine" power,
now calculations began to be undertaken by mine and
factory owners as to how many horses might be dispensed
with by utilizing, for all types of goods transport, this new
form of coal-powered locomotion. Indeed by 1830, with
the opening of the world's first intercity passenger railway
between Liverpool and Manchester (the L&MR), there was
worldwide interest in the possibilities demonstrated by
Britain's new railways. (While the first recorded use of rail
transport in Great Britain was Sir Francis Willoughby's
"Wollaton Waggonway" built in Nottinghamshire between
1603 and 1604 to carry coal, and the first for public use
employing cast iron rails was William Jessop's Wandsworth
to Croydon "Surrey Iron Railway", incorporated in 1799
– the honour of running Britain's first passenger-carrying
public railway goes to the Oystermouth Railway – or
"Mumbles Train" – in South Wales, which was authorised
in 1807. All three lines were initially worked by horses,
and indeed the Surrey Iron Railway remained horse-
drawn throughout its life, from its opening in 1803 until it
was officially closed in 1846.)

*Main: Celebrating the opening of the
Liverpool & Manchester Railway in 1830.*

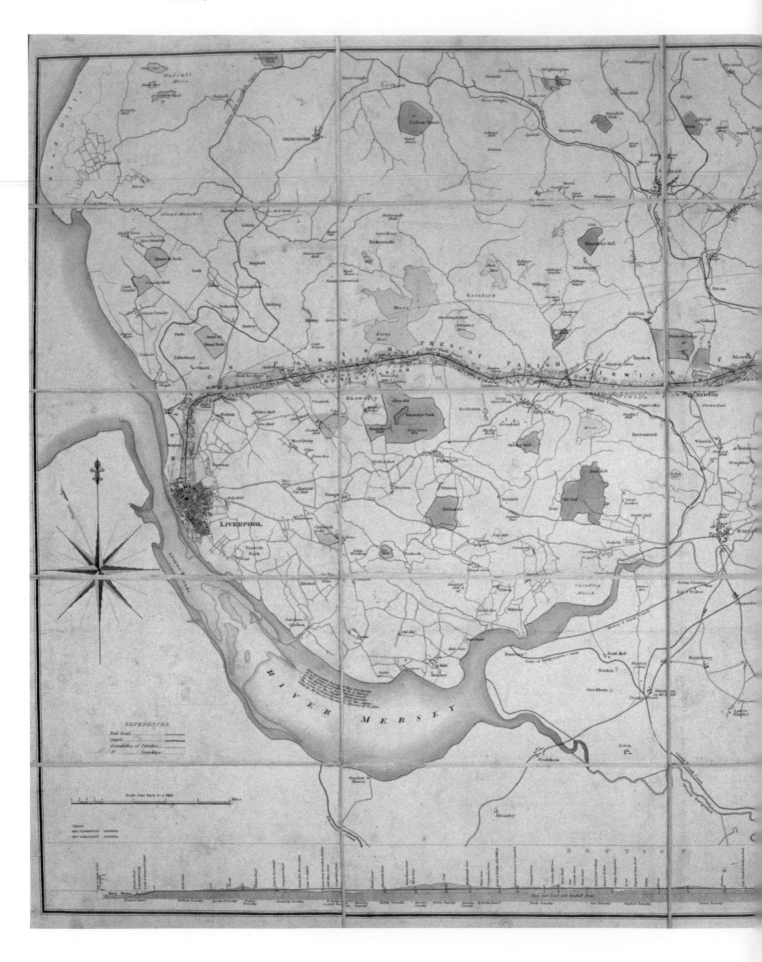

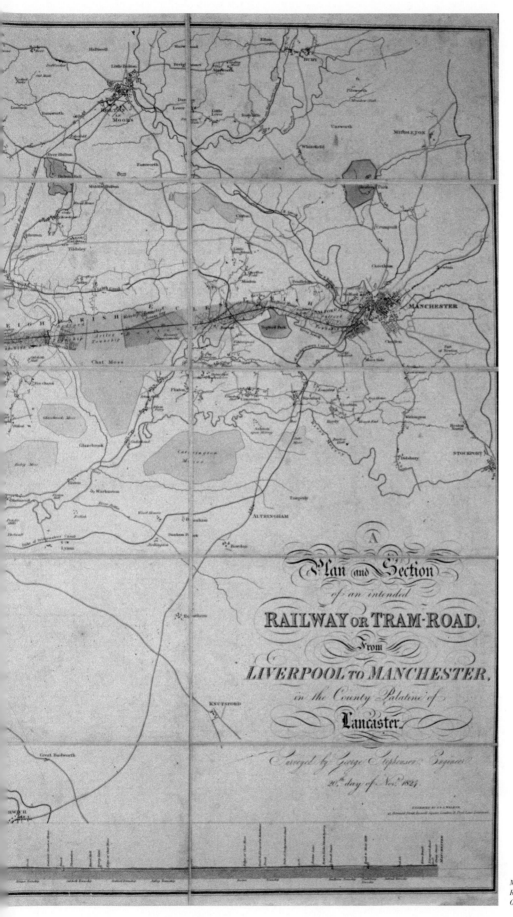

*Main: A map of the Liverpool & Manchester
Railway showing the line as surveyed by
George Stephenson.*

Even in the very early 19th Century, the steam engine historian Robert Stuart tells us that there were already estimated to be "ten-thousand steam engines" in Great Britain. These, of course, were all stationary steam engines, yet said to be doing the "daily labour of more than two hundred thousand horses" – which he equated to as much as that of four and a half million labourers: "an effect," Stuart reported, "greater than the entire manual labour of England." Moreover, steam engines needed "neither rest, nor relaxation". So with the vast majority of improvements to such engines still to come as the 19th Century progressed – not least their transformation to motive power – it is possible to appreciate how, thanks to the adoption of more-and-more advanced steam technology, Britain literally became the economic powerhouse of the world. Steam engines were soon doing work equivalent to many times the population of Great Britain – so enabling and facilitating manufacturing and commercial output of unprecedented proportions.

The Middleton Railway line was also important because it was the first line for which an Act of Parliament was obtained – and so "authorised by Parliament". The Act gave the company power compulsorily to obtain "wayleave" (or right of passage through land not owned by the company, in return for compensation to the landowner). Without the ability to purchase wayleave, the burgeoning rail network of the 19th Century would have been strangled at birth. Middleton was also the first to lay "edge rails" around 1807, made entirely of iron – superseding Richard Trevithick's much weaker cast-iron plated wooden rails, of just a few years earlier.

Very early railways such as the Stockton & Darlington operated much as had the old wagonways – the railway merely owned the tracks, and so anyone who paid an appropriate fee could operate either steam trains or horse-powered wagons on them. As traffic grew, this situation tended to create chaos, and some regulation, scheduling and signalling began to be needed, not least for safety reasons – especially as engines soon became faster. By 1833, only steam engines were permitted on such railways, and parallel tracks were built for trains to travel in both directions without fear of collision. In effect, the Stockton & Darlington Railway was important because it established methods of operating that eventually became commonplace on all railways, not only in Britain but throughout the world. Investors and entrepreneurs took especial note of the Stockton & Darlington Railway's achievements, because it was a great financial success; and they were quite undeterred by any early technical problems (such as the unfortunate boiler explosion in 'Locomotion No 1', which killed its driver in 1828).

Left: Specification of John Birkenshaw's patent for an improvement in the construction of malleable iron rails, 1824.

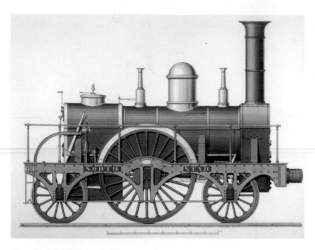

Above: 'North Star' 2-2-2 steam locomotive, 1837.

Being the only engine actually to complete the entire course as specified during the 1829 Rainhill trials, the strengths of Stephenson's 'Rocket' soon became apparent, and it set the template for future locomotive design: instead of the awkward early valve gear, cylinders on each side of the engine drove large wheels more quietly and efficiently through coupling rods (although the cylinders were not yet fully horizontal, as on later locomotives); but inside the boiler was the greatest innovation – the old single flue had become a series of 25 copper pipes that conducted the hot gases, greatly increasing the heating surface. The success of 'Rocket' as a steam engine of clearly-improved design created a demand that ultimately led to the Stephenson Company becoming pre-eminent as builders of steam locomotives, not only in the United Kingdom, but soon throughout Europe and much of America.

Although it was never adopted as the standard, Brunel's preferred "broad gauge" rails (just over seven feet apart, which he claimed were much safer than Stephenson's standard gauge of four feet eight and a half inches), saw the introduction of some powerful engines with huge driving wheels. The first such engine to run on Brunel's Great Western Railway was 'North Star' (ironically built by Robert Stephenson & Co, in Newcastle). On 31 May 1838, 'North Star' made its inaugural journey from Paddington to Maidenhead – which was to be the site of Brunel's impressive new railway viaduct across the Thames (also called the "sounding arch", due to its extraordinary echoes). This viaduct was completed in 1839, and was a wonder of its age, for it consisted of two brick arches that were then the widest and flattest in the world. From 1847, a fleet of magnificent and successful 'Iron Duke' Class 4-2-2 passenger express locomotives became the mainstay of the GWR.

Main: *A steam locomotive crossing the River Thames at Maidenhead. This masonry arch bridge was designed by Isambard Kingdom Brunel and built in 1838.*

Main: Constructing Praed Street (now Paddington)
Station, London, 1866-68.

A further important general innovation was introduced by Matthew Kirtley, chief engineer for the Midland Railway, so that by 1859 all locomotives had adopted an improved design that saw engines burning coal instead of the less efficient and more expensive (but much less smoky) coke – although cleaning of the soot that coal produced was regularly required from then on, and was quite burdensome.

Since there was no coordinated national plan for railway building or railway networks, by 1850 there were, leading into the heart of London, seven great railway termini – the new "cathedrals" of the age of steam. These enormous stations continually disgorged travellers and commuters, and caused chaos by bringing about a relatively new phenomenon: severe traffic congestion. Surprisingly perhaps, from the 1830s – at a time when the first truly viable railway systems and steam engines were just coming into service – there were already proposals to build an underground railway to ease street traffic. In 1854, the Metropolitan Railway was granted permission to build one such line. Steam locomotives, pulling gas-lit wooden carriages, began plying the first route on the new "subterranean railway" between Paddington and Farringdon Street on 10 January 1863. This astonishingly novel type of railway was an instant success, carrying an estimated 38,000 passengers on its opening day, and over nine million in the first year.

SCAN WITH
layar
See page 5
for instructions

Above: The construction work of the Metropolitan Railway (now part of the District and Circle Lines), utilizing the 'cut and cover' technique, caused much disruption to London neighborhoods.

The London "Met" adopted GWR broad gauge locomotives initially, though tunnel ventilation to rid the atmosphere of smoke, soot and steam, was not really adequate for passenger comfort, so Great Northern Line engines were briefly adopted, with little further improvement. In order to solve the pollution conundrum, the Met's chief engineer, Sir John Fowler (1817-98), initially proposed – and in 1861-62 even trialled – a "fireless" locomotive. Although ingenious in concept, Fowler's engine unfortunately had limited success because the condensing system leaked, causing the boiler to run dry.

Fowler's broad gauge 2-4-0 tender locomotive, constructed by Robert Stephenson & Co, was built to work as a normal engine in open railway cuttings, but as soon as it went underground, the firebox would be closed. Internal fire

bricks were then relied upon to act as a heat reservoir, with steam being generated by all the stored heat, and exhaust steam being re-condensed and fed back into the boiler, rather than left to escape. After a failed second trial, the engine – which then came to be known as 'Fowler's Ghost' – was abandoned. The Met soon returned to using condensing steam engines, and a chastened Fowler designed, in 1864, the purpose-built 4-4-0 'A' class tank engines that were later refined and reincarnated as 'B' class engines, running successfully right up to the 1900s – at which time all the lines were electrified.

Fowler's extraordinary career as a civil engineer was ultimately to take him throughout the world – advising on every aspect of railway construction (especially in relation to tunnel and bridge building).

Above: A steam locomotive hauling carriages through an underground tunnel.

While "cut and cover" methods were mostly adopted on the new underground railway, practical difficulties relating to digging up such a busy metropolis, and problems gaining landowner permission, led to the digging of deeper, smaller tunnels. The development of cleaner, electric-powered trains was born out of necessity for running in such deep-level "tubes" (cable-hauling also first being proposed) and, as early as 1890, electric trains appeared on the City & South London Railway's King William Street to Stockwell line – so presaging, even in the late 19th Century, the ultimate superseding of coal-powered steam, in favour of 'healthier' sources of power. What eventually became the complex London Underground Railway system stimulated the growth of the City of London right from its beginnings. It also greatly drove forward the business of the City, which was then the hub of the British Empire (and indeed of world commerce). And in its day, the London Underground was the most extensive subterranean railway network in the world.

Main: Horses pulling carts do their share to assist the labourers during works on the Thames Embankment at Westminster.
Big Ben and the Houses of Parliament can be seen in the distance, looking west from the Charing Cross side.

Main: 271 C1 class engine, circa 1902, complete with
Walschaerts valve gear.

Major innovations in steam engine design from the late 19th Century onwards include a transition from 'simple expansion' type to 'compound' locomotives, which re-used steam a second time by employing both high and low pressure cylinders, so making them more efficient. Compounding was first introduced on 'Experiment' class locomotives of the London & North Western Railway in 1882. And while 'Stephenson's Link Motion' valve gear was highly successful throughout the 19th Century, a significant advance was made by the Belgian Egide Walschaerts (1820-1901) whose reliable, lighter-weight 'Walschaerts valve gear' could be mounted on the outside of the engine frame – better facilitating reverse, and economising on steam.

Walschaerts valve gear subsequently became the standard on many 20th-Century locomotives. Sir Nigel Gresley's more complex 'conjugated valve gear', patented in 1915, was mostly hidden from view when the concept of wind-tunnel tested 'streamlined' locomotives was adopted, such as that used on the LNER Class A4 'Mallard' for its record-breaking run in 1938 – one of the high points of British steam engine design. The evolution of the steam engine and of the steam locomotive had been quite extraordinary, yet it remains a remarkable testament to early modern British engineering that Chinese locomotives built as late as the 1980s still owed much to the fundamental design principles established by Stephenson's famous 'Rocket', as far back as 1829.

Early Engines

Cornishman Richard Trevithick (1771-1833),
an inventor and mining engineer, was to
build the first full-scale working railway
steam locomotive after his development of the
high-pressure steam engine. Born in Illogan,
Redruth, a mile from where his father was a
mine captain, Trevithick developed an affinity
for engineering at an early age. He studied at
Camborne School of Mines, which led to his
heightened interest in mine engineering and his
pioneering career leading up to the age of steam.
He was instrumental in advocating the use of
high-pressure steam as a means to increase the
efficiency of engines pumping water out of tin
and copper mines across the county and his
innovative approach made Cornwall's mining
practices the envy of the world.

*Main: A drainage system invented by English engineer and inventor
Richard Trevithick, for a tin mine circa 1800.*

Above: Richard Trevithick's first passenger-carrying
common road locomotive at Camborne in 1801.

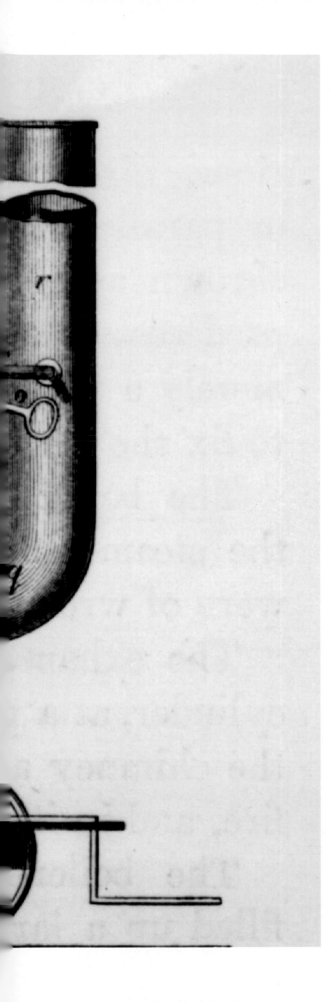

Above: Richard Trevithick.

Trevithick first worked with his father at Wheal Treasury where he made significant improvements to the Bull Steam Engine. This led to a move further west to Penzance, at Ding Dong mine, to become chief engineer, where he developed a high-pressure engine that was extremely successful at raising ore as well as refuse from the depths of the site. As a result, mining across Cornwall and South Wales was greatly transformed and Trevithick pioneered the idea further by developing the first traction engine in 1796. This in turn led to the first steam locomotive and, in 1801, the engineer took a number of friends on an exceptionally short journey, limited mainly because Trevithick couldn't find a way to keep the steam going for any length of time, in a larger modified engine known as the 'Puffing Devil'. However, the features it did have were a cylindrical horizontal boiler with a single horizontal cylinder let into it. The pressure of steam allowed the piston to be propelled back and forth and was, in turn, linked to a piston rod and connecting rod to a crankshaft, which bore a large flywheel.

Two years later, his success was noted in London and investment was made, but later withdrawn following the invention's limitations, from Vivian & West. Serious issues with the engine had prevented it from pulling a carriage and the company was disappointed in the practical outcome and the locomotive's overall shortcomings. Trevithick showed his inventions in London, to fellow Cornishman Humphrey Davy (1778-1829), amongst others, who was knighted for his services to science by George III in 1812. (Interestingly, Davy claimed to be the first inventor of the safety lamp in 1815, the very year that George Stephenson also made the same claim. Many regard Davy as the true inventor of the lamp that became of paramount importance in gassy coalmines although Stephenson's lamp remained in use throughout the North of England.)

Eminent engineer James Watt (1736-1819) dismissed Trevithick's experiments as too risky, and the two men fell out when the Cornish engineer later accused Watt of using his influence in Parliament to ban his experiments in steam locomotives. Watt felt that high temperature steam would lead to disastrous explosions.

Renewed interest and help arrived in the form of Samuel Homfray, a great admirer of Trevithick. Homfray, owner of the Pen-y-darren Ironworks in Merthyr Tydfil, South Wales, commissioned the engineer to redevelop his steam locomotive and even bet owner of the Cyfarthfa Ironworks, Richard Crawshay, 1,000 guineas that he would construct an engine capable of hauling 10 tons of iron along a tramway. It began with Trevithick producing the world's first steam engine in February 1804 with a single vertical cylinder, eight foot flywheel and long piston rod. Homfray won the bet when the Pen-y-darren locomotive – reaching speeds of five miles per hour – pulled ten tons of iron, around 70 passengers and five wagons from the ironworks to the Merthyr-Cardiff Canal. The journey of nine miles was aided by a locomotive, which turned the exhaust steam up the chimney. Trevithick wrote in a letter to Davies Gilbert on 22 February 1804: "Yesterday we proceeded on our journey with the engine. We performed the nine miles in four hours and five minutes. We had to remove some large rocks on the way. On our return home one of the small bolts that fastened the axle to the boiler broke, and all the water ran out of the boiler. Boulton and Watt have strained every nerve to get a bill passed in the House of Commons to stop these engines, saying the lives of the public are endangered."

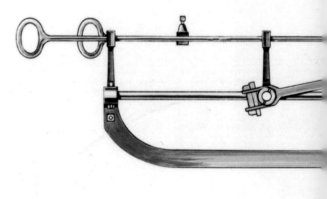

Above: Scottish engineer James Watt.

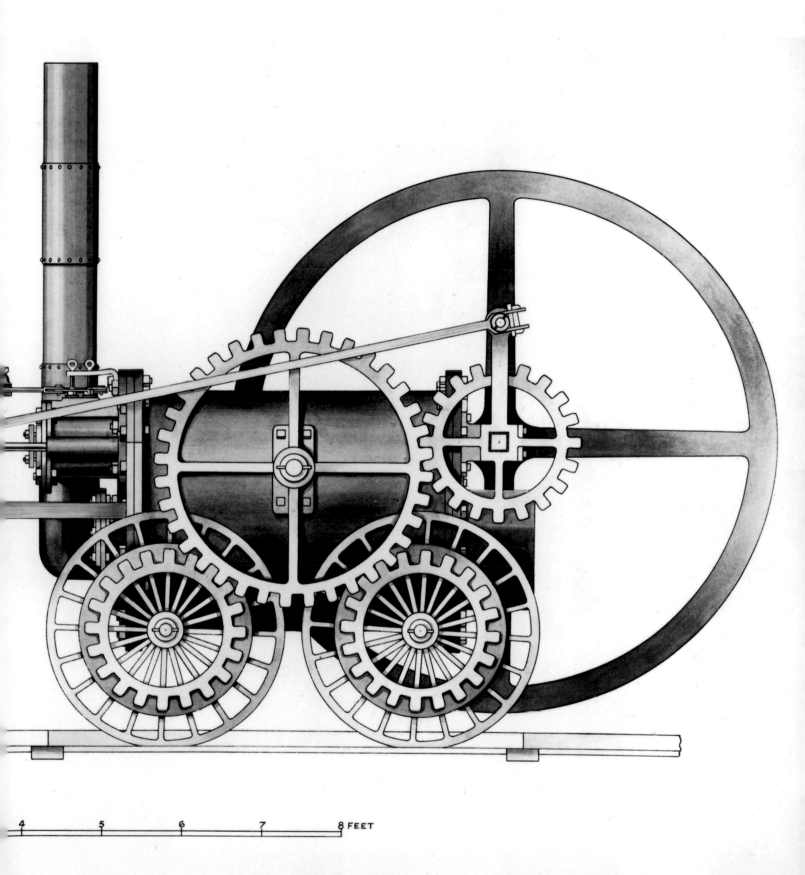

4   5   6   7   8 FEET

Above: A side elevation drawing showing the locomotive designed by Richard Trevithick in 1803 that pioneered the use of high pressure steam.

Above: An advertisement for Richard Trevithick's portable steam engine.

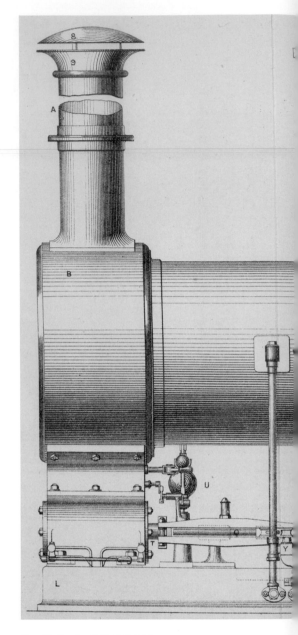

Above: The idea of a portable steam engine became practicable with the introduction of high-pressure non-condensing engines, pioneered by Richard Trevithick in 1802.

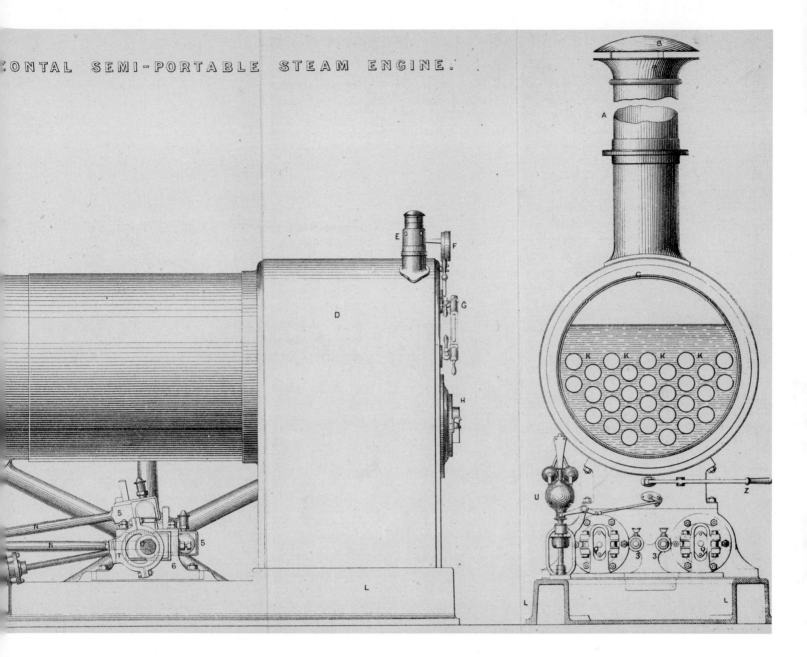

ONTAL SEMI-PORTABLE STEAM ENGINE.

The draught produced the hot gasses from the fire more powerfully through the boiler, but the Pen-y-darren was only to make three journeys. It was simply too heavy for the cast iron rails, which it managed to break on all three outings – cast iron was to prove extremely brittle when it came to heavy locomotives. The seven-ton locomotive, Homfray deduced, was unlikely to reduce his transport costs and he abandoned Trevithick and his invention with regret.

Forced to find alternative employment, Trevithick turned to owner of the Wylam Colliery in Northumberland, Christopher Blackett (1751-1829), who came from a long established mining family. Blackett wanted to develop a steam locomotive that could replace his horse-drawn coal wagons. However, the wooden wagon-way (constructed over five miles in 1748) would prove problematic for the five-ton Wylam locomotive built in 1804, which was just too heavy.

Trevithick returned to Cornwall to experiment further and developed a locomotive called 'Catch Me Who Can'. The locomotive was transported to London and placed on a circular railway around Euston Square in 1808. For one shilling, passengers could enjoy a ride around one of London's more affluent squares during July and August that same year. Reaching speeds of 12 mph, the locomotive was a success, until the rails broke under the weight of the engine. Broken rails and broken down boilers were to hamper Trevithick's career in the United Kingdom.

Above: A steam dredger similar to the one operated by Richard Trevithick.

Disappointingly for Trevithick, his invention was once again abandoned. He was left with no choice but to take employment outside of locomotive construction and development and he found a job using a steam dredger on the Thames where he was paid by the ton to lift waste from the bottom of the river. It was extremely hard work for little reward and, in 1816, he accepted an offer of work in Peru, as an engineer in a silver mine. Here, his steam engines brought him some success and he soon bought his own silver mines. War forced him to leave the country in 1826, having to abandon his successful business and all its assets. He met Robert Stephenson in Colombia, after an unsuccessful stay elsewhere in South America, who gave Trevithick the money to pay for his passage back to Britain. Despite intervention by Robert's father, George Stephenson, on his return Parliament refused to pay Trevithick a pension for all the foundations and blueprints he had laid in steam locomotive design and development. He died in extreme poverty in 1833 and if not for some factory workers who raised the money for a funeral, Trevithick would have been buried a pauper.

Before Trevithick's tragic demise, the first successful steam locomotive was 'Salamanca', a rack railway locomotive built by Matthew Murray (1765-1826) for the narrow gauge Middleton Railway in 1812. Murray, who would become a rival to James Watt and his partner Matthew Boulton (1728-1809) in the race to build steam locomotives, was employed by Marshall, Fenton & Company to develop a flax-spinning machine designed and invented by John Kendrew and Thomas Porthouse, which suffered a number of inefficiencies. Murray successfully solved the problems with the machine and impressed one of his employer's partners, Samuel Fenton, to the point where a new company (Fenton, Murray & Wood) was incorporated.

Left: Richard Trevithick developed this particular high-pressure, non-condensing engine in 1805.

Above: A model of the 'Salamanca' rack locomotive, 1812, that used a rack and pinion system devised by John Blenkinsop (1783-1831).

*Above: Matthew Murray (1765-1826) was an English
manufacturer of steam engines and machine tools.*

The company's engineering works opened next door
to John Marshall's mill in Leeds and both businesses
prospered as a result. It was this that led to Murray's
rivalry with Boulton & Watt, as a leading producer of
steam engines, and John Blenkinsop, from Middleton
Colliery, commissioned the young engineer to build him
an exclusive locomotive. Both men were convinced that
smooth wheels on a smooth rail would not efficiently propel
the locomotive and its load along the track (which was later
disproved by Stephenson). As a result, they came up with
a proposal to use a combination of a locomotive cogwheel
and a toothed rack rail – known as the rack railway. John
Blenkinsop patented the railway in 1811, although it would
never take off commercially.

Their first locomotive was the 'Salamanca' – with cogwheels
– which was inaugurated in June 1812. Three more
locomotives would follow, but the rack railway did not
take off in other collieries. The locomotive, comprising
two vertical cylinders within the top of the boiler and
pistons which drove the rack wheels through the rods and
pinions were heavy on the driving gear wheel. However, the
'Salamanca' was capable, at a speed of 4 mph, of hauling
90 tons. The five-ton locomotive replaced 50 horses and
200 men, but the four engines were expensive. Eventually,
Fenton, Murray & Wood supplied Great Western Railway
(GWR) with locomotives during the 1830s, although they
declined earlier to provide engines for the Stockton &
Darlington Railway.

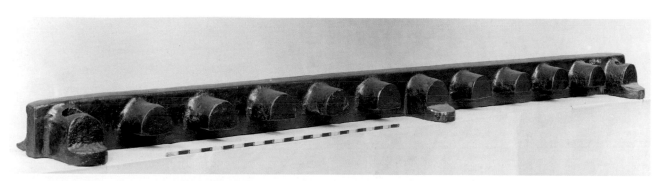

*Above: Replica of a six-foot length of Blenkinsop's rack rail from the
Middleton Colliery line, Leeds, Yorkshire.*

Just two years after the completion of the 'Salamanca' locomotive, Christopher Blackett, alongside William Hedley (1779-1843), his manager, built 'Puffing Billy' in 1814. Hedley became manager at Walbottle Colliery at the tender age of 21 and was spotted by Blackett. Like Trevithick, Hedley's first locomotive, 'Wylam Dilly', was too heavy for the wooden rails at Blackett's colliery. However, in 1808, Blackett replaced the wooden wagon-way with cast iron rails and the steam locomotive "project" was once again underway for the mine owner.

Alongside Hedley worked engine-wright Jonathan Foster and blacksmith Timothy Hackworth. Hedley had the foresight to realize that if the wheels of the locomotive were coupled, then the sheer weight of the engine would provide enough adhesion – the reason why Blenkinsop and Murray developed the rack railway in the first place – and that smooth wheels on a smooth rail would haul freight. He experimented and his findings supported his theory. Hedley applied for a patent and Blackett supplied the rails. All that was needed now was a reliable locomotive.

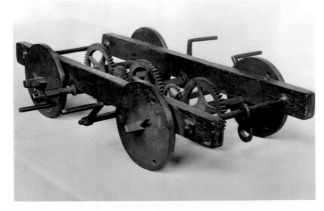

Above: William Hedley built a test carriage in 1812, powered by four men working levers.

*Main: 'Wylam Dilly', built by William Hedley in 1813
for use at Wylam Colliery near Newcastle.*

*Above: 'Puffing Billy' which, together with its sister locomotive
'Wylam Dilly', is the oldest surviving locomotive in the world.*

The 'Wylam Dilly' was joined by 'Puffing Billy' in 1814. 'Puffing Billy' was one of three similar engines built by Hedley at Wylam Colliery. The locomotive was a prototype that was rebuilt in 1815 with 10 wheels (although it was returned to its eight-wheel original form in 1830) – and it remained in service for 48 years until 1862. This locomotive would prove pivotal in the development of steam locomotives the world over with its two vertical cylinders on either side of the boiler. The engine incorporated a number of features – unseen before – including a single crankshaft beneath the frames from which the gears were driven, although the locomotive had some limitations with regard to its technology. Despite the coupled wheels, traction proved difficult when it was discovered that the cast iron rails were just not robust enough to carry the eight-ton engine. Weight was eventually spread more evenly with the introduction of four axles. While the locomotive began with eight wheels – then had 10 – and was reinstated with eight in 1830, the final 'Puffing Billy' was constructed with four wheels. This, together with a newly designed edge rails track made the locomotive more reliable and some of the more serious issues were solved.

The locomotive had a major impact on George Stephenson and played a huge part in the use of steam locomotives in collieries across the country, despite the fact that it was rather slow at 5 mph.

Hedley eventually rented the South Moor Colliery where he developed a steam-powered machine, which developed Trevithick's idea of pumping water out of mines. Hedley's pump from the 1830s was used in collieries across the North of England.

'Puffing Billy' certainly inspired George Stephenson (1781-1848), but he was just as inspired by Richard Trevithick's early locomotives and the work, experiments, and engines built by Murray. However, it was Stephenson himself who would become the pivotal figure in the development and widespread adoption of steam locomotives. His work improved the locomotives of the early pioneers and was instrumental in the locomotives that saw the first public steam railway in the world incorporated – the Stockton & Darlington Railway in 1825. The civil and mechanical engineer was regarded as the "Father of the Railways" and was considered – particularly in the Victorian era – as a high profile pioneer of the modern world. The rail gauge he designed became the world's "standard" gauge (at 4 feet 8.5 inches) and is sometimes dubbed the "Stephenson gauge".

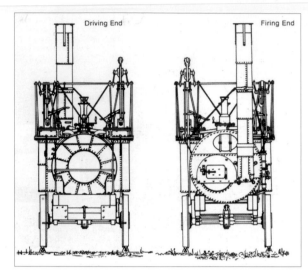

Above and below: Detailed drawing of 'Puffing Billy'.

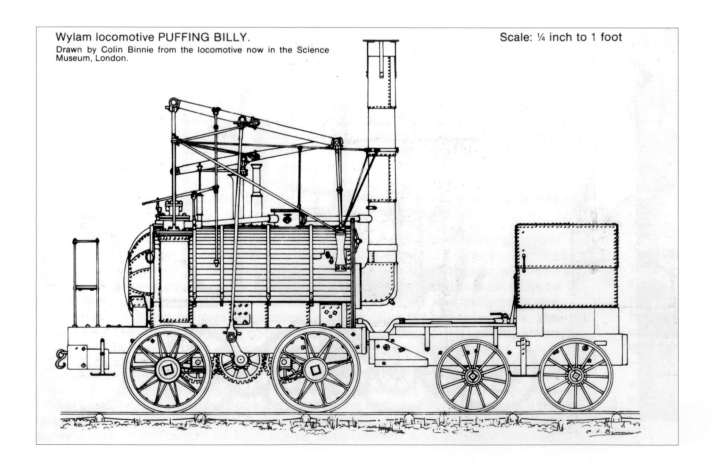

Wylam locomotive PUFFING BILLY.
Drawn by Colin Binnie from the locomotive now in the Science Museum, London.

Scale: ¼ inch to 1 foot

Above: A representation of steam engine pioneer George Stephenson (R) examining 'Puffing Billy'.

Above: Robert Stephenson (1803-59) attained independent fame with his designs for, among others, the Britannia Tubular Bridge and the Royal Border Bridge at Berwick, both constructed in 1850.

Until he was 18 years old, George Stephenson was illiterate. However, he knew the value that an education would give him and paid for his own lessons at night school – as was common among miners. (Today, many local primary schools in existence started as night schools for both coal and iron ore miners.) He worked at Black Callerton Colliery as a brakesman during his early career and, because he was married, mended shoes and clocks to supplement his income. The Stephensons moved to Killingworth when George gained a job – again as a brakesman – in the pit, following the birth of the couple's son Robert in 1803. Stephenson's daughter died a year or so later and, in 1806, his wife died of tuberculosis. He moved to Scotland for a short time, but returned after his father suffered a mining accident. In 1811, when the pumping engine at High Pit, where he now worked, broke down, Stephenson offered to fix it. As a result he was soon made engine-wright for the collieries at Killingworth, which led to his experiences, for the first time with steam-driven engines.

Main: George Stephenson and family with a colliery and early colliery engine in the background.

Stephenson developed a safety lamp in 1815, at the
same time as Davy, but while the Cornishman had the
advantages of a scientific background behind him (and the
support of his peers), the young miner had nothing but
common sense and trial and error to guide him. While the
two ideas differed, Stephenson was accused of "poaching"
his invention from Davy – probably due to his lowliness
in the eyes of the scientific authorities, and it made him
determined that his son, Robert Stephenson, would receive
the best education possible. He was eventually exonerated
and award £1,000 (Davy received £2,000), although his
rival went to his grave believing his idea had been stolen.
Stephenson's lamp – known as the Geordie Lamp – was
used in the North of England, while Davy's was popular in
all other regions of Britain. It is believed that this is how
the term "Geordie" was coined. When Trevithick visited
Tyneside and built a locomotive there, many engineers
were inspired and built engines of their own. Stephenson
was one such engineer who built his first locomotive in
1814. He named it 'Blücher' and designed it to haul coal on
the Killingworth wagon-way.

*Left: George Stephenson and his
son Robert at work together in their
cottage, circa 1820.*

Above: 0-4-0 locomotive 'Locomotion No 1' was built by George Stephenson in 1825
and was used on the Stockton & Darlington Railway, the first public railway.

The flanged-wheel adhesion locomotive was constructed in the colliery workshop and proved it could haul 30 tons of coal at 4 mph. Its success would lead to 15 further locomotives at the colliery, where most were built for Killingworth and the Hetton Colliery Railway. While wooden rails were proving inadequate for steam locomotives and were, essentially, on the way out, cast iron also had its problems. Stephenson, alongside William Losh, improved the brittleness displayed in cast iron rails by experimenting with a "steam spring" which cushioned the weight of the locomotive, through steam pressure. By the time he was designing locomotives for the Stockton & Darlington Railway, Stephenson had revised his plans and resorted to wrought iron rails, which would lead to a life-long rift with Losh.

Just before this, however, Stephenson was instrumental in the first ever railway that didn't require any animal power at all when he was commissioned to build eight miles of track for the Hetton Colliery Railway. 'Locomotion' – or 'No 1 Engine' – was designed (although it was originally called 'Action') and built for the Stockton & Darlington Railway, which was incorporated in a Parliamentary Bill in 1821. Covering a 25-mile stretch, the railway linked a number of collieries from Bishop Auckland, through Darlington and on to the River Tees at Stockton. Stephenson, assisted by Robert Stephenson surveyed the line and construction began that same year. Robert Stephenson and Company was established by George Stephenson, and director of the Stockton & Darlington Railway Edward Pease. Together with partner, Michael Longridge, from Bedlington Ironworks, they began business in earnest.

'Locomotion' was an improved design from Stephenson's earlier locomotives at Killingworth. There was high-pressure steam from a centre-flue boiler, a chimney that contained a steam-blast, which drove two vertical cylinders, which in turn were contained within the boiler. Above this was a pair of yokes to transmit the power downwards, through pairs of connecting rods. It was one of the very first locomotives to have coupling rods to link its 0-4-0 wheels rather than chains or gears and it would become one of the first locomotives to run a passenger service. With the advent of locomotives, such as the 'Rocket', with its improved advances in design, 'Locomotion' quickly became obsolete. It had, however, provided a much-needed prototype, and remained in service until 1841. Sixteen years later, 'Locomotion' was preserved and put on display. It is part of the National Collection and can be seen at the Darlington Railway Centre and Museum.

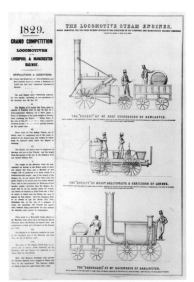

'Locomotion' was followed by a number of locomotives
including 'Hope', 'Diligence' and 'Black Diamond' and
the Stockton & Darlington Railway was opened in
September 1825. Stephenson drove 'Locomotion' on its
first journey for the company and gained speeds of up to
24 mph while hauling an 80-ton load for two hours over
a distance of nine miles. This inaugural trip was also the
first time that passengers were included – 'Locomotion'
also hauled a purpose-built carriage with invited guests,
including the actress and writer Fanny Kemble. Through
experience gained on the Stockton & Darlington Railway,
Stephenson was able to carefully survey the line that was
to open between Liverpool and Manchester just five years
later. The line was completed – after careful and often
problematic construction – in 1829 and the Rainhill Trials
were organized by the L&MR management to ascertain
who would build the locomotives for the railway.

Above: The Stockton & Darlington Railway opened on 27 September 1825.

Obviously, George Stephenson wanted to enter the competition and his locomotive 'Rocket' was born. It was designed entirely as a passenger locomotive and closely adhered to the rules of the competition. 'Rocket' was also the first locomotive to bring innovations together and, as a result, was to prove the most advanced locomotive of its day – it was to become such a famous design that it was used as a template for many steam locomotives for the next 150 years. Speed and reliability were paramount when it came to 'Rocket's design and it was required to haul three times its own weight. Stephenson set about designing a new lightweight engine, built for speed which incorporated a single pair of driving wheels – it was the first 0-2-2 – which gave it a number of advantages. These included the second axle, which was smaller and more lightweight and 2.5 tons of its total weight were placed on the driving wheels. While Stephenson was pivotal

in 'Rocket's design, he was largely away building the Liverpool & Manchester Railway and it was Robert, who had returned from South America, who was on site while the locomotive took shape. Henry Booth, a senior manager at the Liverpool & Manchester Railway, should also be noted for his innovative advice and suggestions when it comes to the design of this locomotive.

Entries could weigh up to six tons and had to be capable of travelling for a distance of 60 miles. Robert Stephenson (although in South America for a time where he met Trevithick) was in charge of the design and, encouraged by Henry Booth, he opted for the French-designed, fire-tube boiler. This improved heat exchange was a significant innovation and 'Rocket' proved an outright winner. The only downside to a celebratory day at the grand opening of L&MR in September 1930 was the death of MP for Liverpool, William Huskisson, who died of his injuries after being struck by 'Rocket'.

Stephenson's reputation, nevertheless, was firmly established and his place in the history books assured. He was also responsible for the skew bridge idea and the first of its kind (to be built at an angle) was constructed in 1830 in Rainhill over the railway. Following all his pioneering successes, many leading engineers and mechanics from all over the world came to visit Stephenson and to learn from the most influential man in steam locomotive history, however, some of his successors felt that he was outdated when it came to civil engineering. Stephenson's preference for the traditional was often cited as being too costly and time consuming. His reluctance to "cut corners" would lose him some railway construction jobs, but his reputation meant that he was never short of offers either. These early engines sparked a public interest that would last through the Golden Age of Steam and into the 21st Century.

Above: Stephenson's 'Rocket'.

Above: 'Rocket' comes in first at the trials competition held at Rainhill Bridge, 1829.

Above: "Rain, Steam and Speed", 1844, Turner.

While the newspapers were quick to comment on railway developments and all the benefits that came with them, other commentaries were also taking shape and some didn't happen with words. High profile artists of the time, including Joseph Mallard William Turner (1775-1851), had much to "say" when it came to the railways and the development of steam. In a painting entitled "Rain, Steam and Speed – The Great Western Railway" (1844), Turner created an illustrious work of the Maidenhead Railway Bridge, across the Thames – between Maidenhead and Taplow. Built to the design of Isambard Kingdom Brunel, the bridge is represented by cool colors applied with rapid brushstrokes over the surface of the canvas. It gives the painting the appearance of surrounding the subject in a misty haze. The painting came at a time when the railways were beginning to gain a stronghold in the British countryside. They enabled progress, communication and business and artists were keen to convey how steam and speed were gradually taking over from nature. Turner's 1844 painting gave a romanticized view of the blossoming modern world, but he wasn't the only artist to want to share his thoughts on progress.

Above: Stephenson's 'North Star' steam engine, 1837.

Above: An early English steam locomotive hauling a tender and three carriages adapted from horse-drawn coaches.

Paul Cézanne was also interested in portraying the changing world brought about by the advent of steam, however, he was more interested in landscape compositions, which incorporate the railways and their infrastructure, rather than painting the locomotives themselves. In a painting dated circa 1870 entitled "The Railway Cutting", he depicts the effects that the landscape endured in order to accommodate the new innovative technology. His painting shows the railway cutting at the centre of the piece complete with signal box. Monet and Manet were other high profile artists who showed an interest and provided commentary on the arrival of steam locomotives. George Walker was the first artist to paint a steam locomotive when he visited Middleton Colliery – run by Murray and Blenkinsop in 1814.

Above: George Walker's "The Collier" (1814) features the earliest known representation of a steam train ('Salamanca') on the Leeds & Middleton Railway.

A New Way To Travel

Great Britain was the first nation to build an extensive canal network for industrial purposes. It was the envy of the world and would play a pivotal role in Britain's Industrial Revolution, by emerging just as mud tracks and pack-horses began to disappear. By the 1770s, canals were enjoying their "Golden Age", but change came in the first half of the 1800s with the development of steam. From about 1840, railways began to dominate. They were faster, could carry significantly more freight and a shift in investment from boats to locomotives meant that a new revolution was on the way.

O ver the following 10 years, the railways became well established. By comparison, the once thriving waterways started an inevitable decline. Canal companies had little choice but to slash their prices, boatmen had no option but to house their families aboard their vessels, due to losses in wages, and cargo carried on canals dropped to a third of its former glory. In addition, canals were prone to freezing during the winter months and running dry in the summer – they just didn't offer the same reliability as their new competitor. Steam power was tough competition and many struggling canal companies were bought by the railway companies often in a tactical move to gain an advantage over their competitors. Other canals were bought in order to adapt their purpose completely – with a sophisticated network already in place, it made sound business sense to convert a number of waterways ready for tracks and the locomotives and carriages they carried. However, it wasn't just the canals that suffered from the innovations in steam power – mail coaches, which traditionally were an expensive form of transport, also came under threat. Steam locomotives were not only about to change the way that goods were transported, but also the way in which people travelled around the country. Steam was cheaper, and faster. However, that was far from the end of the revolution about to take place.

*Main: An ancient method of transport meets the future as a steam train of
the Liverpool & Manchester Railway crosses the Sankey Valley viaduct near
Warrington, Cheshire while a sailing vessel passes below.*

Left: Remains of the granite troughs that were used as rails by ponies to haul trucks of granite from the quarries at Hay Tor on Dartmoor.

Richard Trevithick's steam locomotive, built in 1804 and trialled at the Pen-y-darren Ironworks in Wales, undoubtedly paved the way for more advanced engineering and the introduction of steam, but his engine was extremely slow and unreliable. Improving on the blueprint set down by Trevithick, John Blenkinsop added a new dimension in 1811 with the introduction of cogs attached to the wheels of the engine, which facilitated a greater grip on the additional rail laid down alongside the earlier rails on which horses had pulled cart loads. A horse pulling a wagon along the "roads", or wagon-ways, such as they were, could manage about half a ton while travelling up to 10 miles in one day. Once rails were introduced – many of which were laid in former canals – a single horse could manage a wagon carrying around two tons and cover an impressive distance of 20 miles per day. Steam locomotives, combined with the additional grip of Blenkinsop's cogs, could manage a staggering 200 miles while pulling 40 tons. William Hedley's 'Puffing Billy' made its debut in 1813 and proved so reliable that it was to remain in operation for 50 years, but as described in the section on Early Engines, it was George Stephenson who would truly revolutionise the new way to travel.

SCAN WITH
layar
See page 5
for instructions

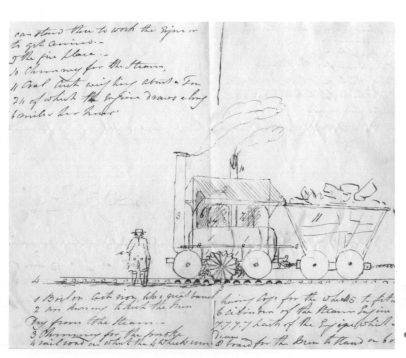

Above: A letter from Mr Leighton Dalrymple explaining his visit to Wakefield and Leeds, including a description and sketch of John Blenkinsop's steam locomotive 'Salamanca', 1812.

Above: The rack rail and driving wheel designed by John Blenkinsop in 1811 consisted of a cogwheel on the locomotive which locked into special teeth in a rack on one side of the rail.

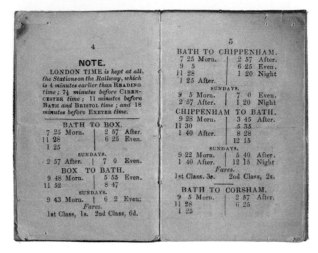

*Above: An early railway timetable with reference to London Time.
Bradshaw's Railway Guide began around 1840 and was the
precursor to today's National Railway timetables.*

The railways would change society forever. Travelling
by train was 50 per cent cheaper than coaches, despite
the enormous investment needed to manufacture and lay
the rails, and further aspects that would change the face
of society were soon to arise. One down side was that
stagecoaches would go out of business, as would many
of the inns and taverns that had previously supported
the horse-fuelled industry. The Industrial Revolution
saw an increase in jobs and wages, which in turn led to
more people having the opportunity to take day trips
and holidays. However, it should be remembered that to
begin with, not everyone could actually afford to travel by
train. It took a while for ticket prices to reach a level that
allowed greater numbers of passengers aboard. Having
a timetable for passengers became a prerequisite and
meant that time had to be quickly standardised across the
country. Whereas any time of day could differ from region
to region, and even town to town, before the railways,
it soon became apparent that all towns, cities and rural
areas needed to run by the same clock if timetabling was
to work effectively.

Main: *This illustration perfectly depicts the demise of travel by coach in favour of the railways.*

Above: Extending the railways made seaside excursions available to the masses.

The fact that locomotives could travel such great distances in a day also saw a dramatic increase in the distribution of newspapers and other forms of written communication to a widespread audience. This is turn led to more people learning to read. Fresh produce, once an ad-hoc luxury for many, suddenly became available on a daily basis, adding to the general health and wellbeing of the nation. Meat, bread, vegetables and milk could now be enjoyed fresh on a daily basis. It is mooted that fish and chips, once confined to seaside resorts, became a national dish after the railways enabled the timely transportation of fresh fish. Politics was also greatly affected by the railways. No longer were the affairs of the country confined solely to the corridors of Parliament. With the advent of steam, messages were spread far and wide on a rapid scale with business leaders and politicians having access to a faster way to travel. Interestingly, urbanization was to grow in a way that was unheard of … and previously unrealized. Bricks and stone could be transported on a grand scale, which led to increased building activities and housing. Stone slabs were cut and transported hundreds of miles from their origin in order to pave Britain's towns and cities.

Main: Fresh produce is unloaded in Glasgow during the 1830s.

Main: Railway companies' plans for expansion have been continuously dogged by environmental issues from the outset with fears often raised about how it would affect the local wildlife. This train is making its way through the spectacular scenery of the North Yorkshire Moors.

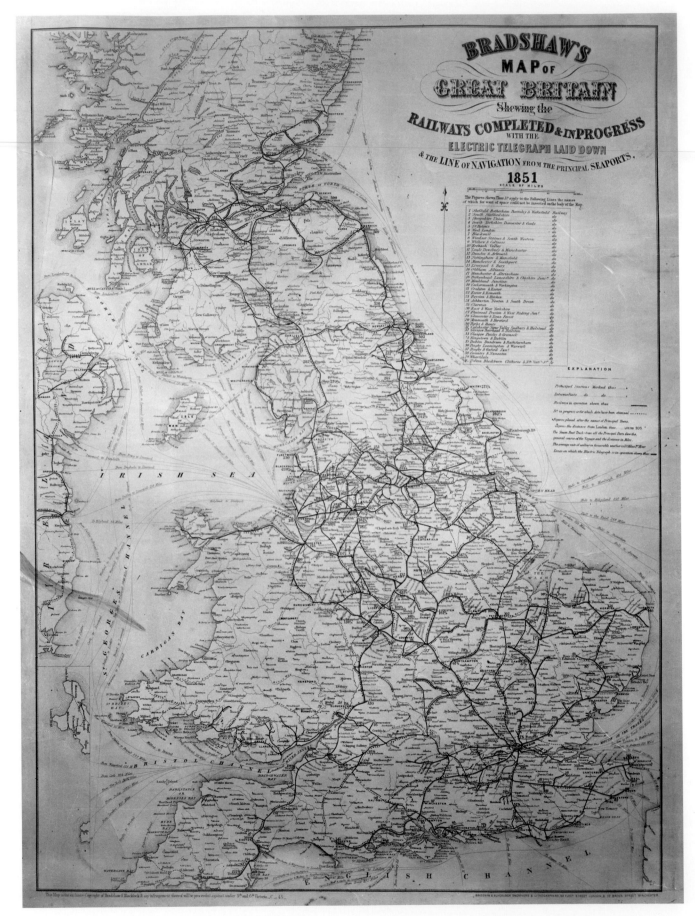

Above: George Bradshaw's map of 1851 shows how the railway network has expanded rapidly.

Above: A broad gauge locomotive designed by Sir Daniel Gooch in 1847.

While improvements were gradual in some ways, and other industries suffered greatly when the railways arrived, they enabled a greater freedom for the country's population. The first locomotives and their freight were initially intended as a means by which to increase business ventures – both domestically and internationally – stretching across the country and reaching the ports. They were also envisaged as a way of helping the economy of Britain to grow and prosper. Passengers were not at the top of the agenda for the railway companies at the outset, but it soon became clear that people were clamoring to be able to travel on these new go-faster "beasts". The railways were set to become the "heartbeat" of the United Kingdom.

To begin with, there were concerns about whether a human being could actually travel at high speeds (around 60 mph) without suffering some intolerable or permanent side affects. What if they couldn't breathe? What about their eyes and ears? Would they cope? There was a real fear that people would be somehow injured or permanently scarred if they travelled on a train. The concept might have seemed exciting and unbelievable but it also provoked real worries and concerns, not just for the health and wellbeing of those willing to undertake a journey but the wildlife and domestic animals close to the paths of the newly created routes.

While the Stockton & Darlington line was the first to open (in 1825), it was the freight line between Liverpool and Manchester that was deemed one of the most significant railways when it opened in 1830, following Stephenson's Rainhill Trials a year earlier. By this time, the Industrial Revolution was craving greater efficiency in its demand for cotton and raw materials for the Lancashire mills and the overcrowding on narrow roads meant that the railway was the only viable option if demands were to be met and progress made. For passengers, the lure of a journey that took just a few hours at 30 mph compared with a 31-mile walk or an uncomfortable coach trip (which lasted many more hours), proved too much. Within months of the line opening, passengers were demanding tickets to travel, much to the surprise of the railway.

Above: Opened on 15 September 1830, the line between Liverpool and Manchester was 31 miles (50 km) long and was the world's first intercity railway.

Main: At the opening of the Stockton & Darlington Railway on 27 September 1825, large crowds saw Stephenson at the controls of 'Locomotion', the locomotive built for the railway by Robert Stephenson & Co, as it pulled 36 wagons to the Stockton terminus.

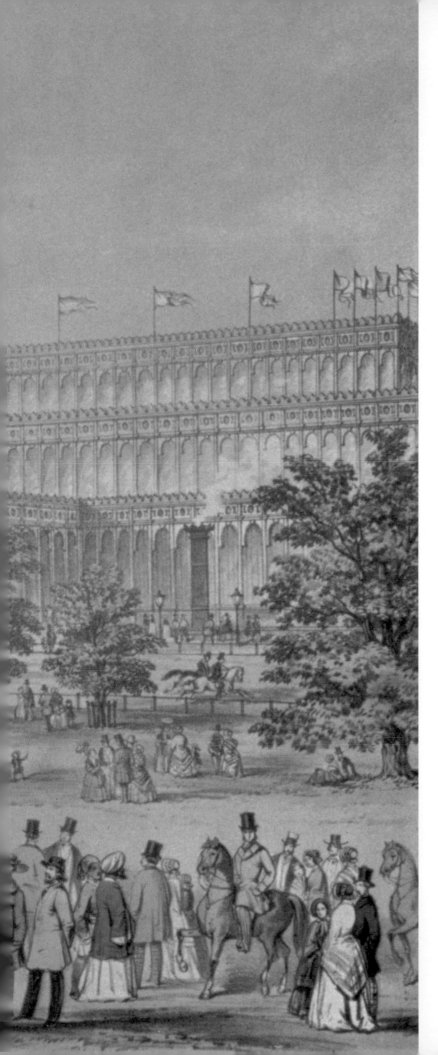

Frances Anne Kemble (27 November 1809 – 15 January 1893) was to do much to persuade people that the railways were safe to travel. Fanny, as she was known, belonged to the famous theatrical Kemble family and was a popular writer about travel, alongside plays and poetry – her memoirs were eventually published in 11 volumes. George Stephenson may have been a brusque engineer, but he was also extremely shrewd and he invited Fanny Kemble to travel by train on the Liverpool & Manchester line. Kemble wrote with wonder about the journey, which persuaded the masses that train travel was not only safe but magical and revolutionary. While on a theatrical tour of the United States, Kemble travelled to Quincy in 1833 where she witnessed the country's first commercial railroad – the Granite Railway. She became a great advocator of rail travel and this provided rail promoters with a powerful "marketing" tool.

The Great Exhibition was held at the "Crystal Palace" in London's Hyde Park in 1851. The glass building – which later moved further south east, outside central London, giving the area where it settled its name – saw around one third of Britain's population visit its thousands of exhibits. Most had travelled to Hyde Park by train. It showed the extent of the enormity of the revolution that the railways had brought about. As a result of the Great Exhibition, towns and villages began to organise "Exhibition Clubs" which travelled to London. Many were travelling by train for the first time and a growth in the economy through travel began.

Main: Crowds – many of whom had travelled by train – gathering outside the Crystal Palace in Hyde Park, London, designed by Sir Joseph Paxton for the Great Exhibition of 1851.

From 1840, the railways had begun to take shape and, by 1855, Britain had a core network of lines extending into Scotland, through the west, east, London, the south east, Wales, Devon and Cornwall. In 1844, Gladstone's Railway Act ensured that each day, there was at least one train that was affordable for the populous. Costing no more than one penny a mile on designated trains, people were able to visit different places across the country and major cities became popular with those that had never experienced the hustle and bustle of "city" life before. Another destination that found its popularity through the railways was the seaside. With affordable travel available day trips became possible. Living standards were rising and the 6,000 miles of railways saw annual passenger numbers reaching into many millions by the middle of the 1850s. Demand for railway companies saw the country flourish in a way that had been unthinkable before. Companies grew – with the need for locomotives and rails, while other companies sprang up in order to maintain them. Banks were required to lend huge amounts of money in order to facilitate construction and maintenance, and they too reaped the rewards. Railway shares on the Stock Exchange became big business and huge manufacturing firms were required to build the engines and rolling stock.

Main: This lattice girder viaduct, supported by cast iron piers, was designed by Thomas Bouch for the South Durham & Lancashire Union Railway's line between Barnard Castle and Tebay (usually known as the Stainmore Route).

Above: The Royal Albert Bridge – linking Cornwall and Devon over the River Tamar – was built by Sir Isambard Kingdom Brunel and was opened by HRH Prince Albert in May 1859.

Above: The Britannia Tubular Bridge (crossing the Menai Straits) was designed by Robert Stephenson (1803-1859) and completed in 1850.

Main: Navvies posing during construction of the almost 1.75 mile long Dove Holes tunnel, circa 1862. The Midland Railway's (MR) Rowsley to Buxton extension line was built to connect the MR system with Manchester and although only 13 miles long its construction took four years.

Above: Running from Curzon Street Station, Birmingham, to Euston Station, London, the 112 mile London & Birmingham Railway (LBR) took 20,000 men nearly five years to build, at a cost of £5.5 million and opened in September 1838.

One of the most important aspects of the railway revolution was the men who built them. Despite living in appalling, cramped conditions, often exploited and cheated by their employers, navvies were fundamental to the development of the railway. This elite workforce was unlike all other manual workers in Britain and prided themselves on their strength. In the 1840s, there were around 200,000 navvies working across the country, building 20,000 miles of railway. To become a navvy, it was imperative to be able to consume huge amounts of food and vast quantities of alcohol – they were often partly paid in beer – in order to build up the strength required for the job. A navvy had to be able to eat two pounds of beef a day and drink a gallon of beer, such was the exertion of building the lines. These proud men, unsurprisingly, had a lower life expectancy than many and were not expected to reach their fifties. Thousands died while building the railways – either through exhaustion or recklessness (a large number of navvies took huge risks). The Settle to Carlisle Line, completed in 1875, was built through extremely harsh terrain and was one of the hardest lines to build as the cemeteries around the area testify. More than half of the lines built by this incredible workforce survive into the 21st Century and are a true legacy to the brave and fearless navvies.

Above: The Great Northern Railway's (GNR) main route from London to Doncaster was completed in 1852, the same year that the railway's London terminus opened at Kings Cross. The railway operated services to many of the major towns in the north of England.

Another way of life that was greatly affected by the railway revolution was football. The oldest club in Britain, Notts County, was formed in 1862. Queen's Park, founded on the south side of Glasgow came in 1867 and did something remarkable – it organized the first international football match ever, between Scotland and England in 1872. Many football clubs were actually established from teams comprising railway workers and it was only natural that the steam revolution would lead to travelling players and fans. It opened up a sport that had its origins in medieval times, and saw the inaugural FA Cup – the first organized competition – played in the 1871-72 season. This in turn led to the formation of the Football League in 1888 and a national sport, already born, was firmly established. From the late 1860s the modern game began to evolve, when a "loose" offside rule was introduced in 1867.

While many believe that the "corner shop" suffered its decline during the 1990s and into the 21st Century with below cost-pricing from major "predatory" supermarkets, it actually began much earlier in the 1850s (although corner shops had enjoyed a resurgence by the mid-1900s). The advent of the railway saw many shun what was on offer in their local shops in order to travel to major cities and sample the goods in burgeoning department stores. Selfridges offered more high end goods in London, for example, while Frank Woolworth created affordable goods for the masses in stores which would eventually cover the country.

Above: Several of today's professional football clubs – Manchester United and Crewe Alexandra to name but two – owe their heritage to railway workers such as this Great Western Railway team who played in their leisure time.

Above: London stores like Selfridges understood the value of the railways in bringing customers to their door and were happy to reciprocate. Here two ladies are using a tube ticket dispensing machine in the department store.

The railways began to branch out – literally – as smaller towns and villages "cried out" to be connected to the network. Local business people often enabled these "branch" lines to be built and, by the end of the 1800s, communities across Britain celebrated the arrival of the railway. Jobs in local areas were created – with station staff being employed – and workmen's trains were added around the home counties, allowing people to travel into London to work. The way in which this took off in the 1860s was unprecedented. Soon, workmen's trains began appearing into other major cities including Manchester and Birmingham.

Prior to 1923, there were more than 300 companies operating on the rail network. Image was everything, from the locomotives and carriages down to the station facilities and the staff that ran them. It was the station that provided passengers with their first impressions of the rail company with whom they travelled and station staff were pivotal in providing a first class service. Working on the railways was a way of life to the staff lucky enough to be employed by a rail company and great pride was taken in station buildings, which were considered much more than just bricks and mortar. It was here that tickets were booked and paid for, timetables could be surveyed and enquiries answered. The station was also somewhere to relax before a journey, long or short, and luggage, often big and bulky, needed to be handled with care. It was here too that the all-important newspapers could be bought, which would encourage a nation to read and take an interest in current affairs, locally, nationally and internationally. It was also the place where books could be bought as newsstands within stations developed. While it may not have come until later – in 1935 – Exeter station became the inspiration for worldwide high-quality paperback publishing and the advent of Penguin Books. The Managing Director of Bodley Head Publishers, Allan Lane, stood on the platform in Exeter that year and searched for something decent to read on his journey back to London. He was disappointed to find that apart from the popular magazines of the day, the only available books were poor-quality paperbacks. With his choice severely limited, Lane made it his mission to change the face of literature available to railway travellers and founded Penguin Books, to provide intelligent travellers with a good read at an attractive price. He advocated that the books he published should be available in tobacconists and newsstands as well as bookshops and should cost no more than a packet of cigarettes. His misfortune while standing on the platform in 1935 would revolutionise the world of publishing.

*Main: Workmen arriving at Victoria Station after travelling on the London Chatham-Dover Railway
with an experimental weekly workmen's ticket costing 1 penny.*

Above: Staff members were extremely proud of their railway station and always did their utmost to maintain its appearance to the highest standard as shown here at Carshalton in south London, circa 1880.

Above: The station walls are covered in posters, advertising everything from sherry to medical remedies and magazines. Allowing businesses to advertise in rail stations had the mutually beneficial effect of bringing revenue to the railway companies and sales to the businesses.

Above: A porter directing a passenger on the platform of a station on the outskirts of Liverpool at the end of the 19th Century.

Alongside bookstalls, bars were a later addition to the station facilities and larger buildings would often house kiosks selling tobacco, sweets, flowers and even fruit. Buildings were often built with elaborate architecture – particularly in larger cities – but this rarely mattered to those who demanded to know why their train was late, or why they needed to change more than once. Passengers were reliant on the patience, knowledge and expertise of the staff at each and every station to allay their concerns and provide them with not just answers, but a relaxing and pleasant experience from the moment they left one destination to the moment they reached another.

The station-master was the most important and high profile member of the railway staff. It was vital that this knowledgeable man was not just visible, but hands-on and capable of dealing with a variety of responsibilities, often simultaneously. Much of what was required of the station-master was dictated by the size of the station, the number of passengers expected, the volume of locomotives through the station and responsibility – even in smaller, rural stations – was high. Smaller stations may have had smaller volumes of passengers, but it was likely that freight trains delivering to local businesses were key to the economic survival of the line and the station. It fell to the station-master to know what the needs of his local area were. He was also responsible for all station staff as well as engine crews and it was his job to set regulations and standards. Unsurprisingly, standards were high and expectations were great. Safety and security were paramount and came under the remit of this pivotal figure.

Right: Everyone wanted to be a train driver! King George tries his hand at driving GWR No 4082 'Windsor Castle' on a visit to Swindon Works in April 1924. Beside him are Queen Mary, the Chairman of the GWR, the General Manager and the Chief Mechanical Engineer.

Workers considered it a privilege to work for a railway company, despite the long hours – often 12 hours a day – and lack of holiday. (It was usual to take only two or three days as annual leave.) Locomotive drivers and their trusted firemen often worked 15 hours a day, yet these roles were coveted. They would remain so, well into the middle of the 20th Century. Even as late as the 1960s and 1970s, many young boys yearned to be train drivers when they grew up.

The position was held in high esteem and employees were prepared to work their way through the ranks, often earning less than £1.25 a week (by the turn of the 20th Century). Drivers and firemen could expect the occasional Sunday off, although platelayers and gangers had shorter working days and most Sundays were a day of rest. However, should problems arise on the line, they were expected back to work immediately.

Above: A Midland Railway worker opening the smoke box door of a steam locomotive in 1904. The locomotive has just stopped since the box is still full of smoke from the fire.

Above: Pullman cars were first used in Britain in 1874. The luxury Pullman car, American in origin, was a railway carriage with a very comfortable interior, furnished as a lounge. Pullmans also had sleeping cars and passengers were served drinks and meals at their seats.

Above: Early dining cars were exclusively for the upper classes and oozed opulence. This is the dining saloon carriage on the 'Ocean Express' from Fishguard in September 1909.

Ticket inspectors had a fairly "easy" working life with shorter days and most weekends free. Being employed by a railway company was considered a "safe" job in terms of having "a job for life" and there was much pride amongst employees.

While every effort was made to ensure that passengers were safe and well looked after, and that station buildings offered all the "modern" facilities available, the actual travel itself was often uncomfortable. To begin with, there were many who did not trust the concept of this "thundering" innovation through the countryside (although attitudes obviously did begin to change). There were still those reluctant to travel on a long journey relatively quickly. Society, at this time, was divided into a three-tier class system. Tickets for first and second class were available, but the working classes were not

offered an affordable ticket until the latter half of the 19th Century. Third class was introduced, eventually, during the Victorian era and classes were divided into upper, middle and lower. Coaches were not originally designed with comfort in mind and third, or lower class, offered a true test in endurance. Open wagons were used and a bumpy ride was inevitable. Only prolonged delays or a downpour could make it any worse. Standards – despite being high across many facets – were still mixed between the rail companies and basic facilities on board would remain unrealized for the best part of 40 years. However, in the 1870s, conditions slowly improved with the introduction of sleeper cars on London & North Western Railway. The Great Northern Railway – between Leeds and London's King's Cross – introduced the first dining car (separated from the other cars to maintain its exclusivity).

Above: The interior of a London, Midland & Scottish Railway (LMS) carriage corridor finished in American black walnut.

Midland Railway was the first company to champion better conditions for third class passengers and advocated from 1872 that these passengers were welcome on all services. The company then abolished middle class and slashed its prices for first class tickets. Before the amalgamation of the railways in 1923, the competition between rail companies was fierce. It soon became clear that in order to compete economically, the passengers had to come first. Corridor trains were introduced in 1891 by Great Western Railway – this led to increased comfort for passengers generally and by 1914 and the advent of World War I passenger trains were more than bearable.

Main: While conditions were improving, the added complication of industrial action meant that passengers were forced to use any means to get home after a hard day's work during this railway strike at Forest Gate Station in October 1919.

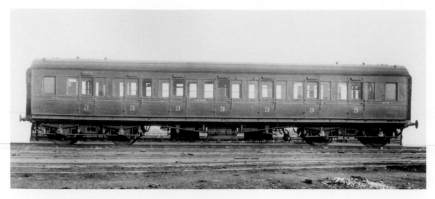

Above: A third class Glasgow & South Western Railway (GSWR) carriage.

Up to this point, the extending of the railway network had continued to a degree, but the building of better roads – initially for lorries and later, cars – saw companies struggling to make significant profits. Despite being consolidated following the First World War (or Great War as it was known at the time), competition from other forms of travel was rife. At the same time, the railways suffered from under investment (for the first time in their history) and a real sense that there was a lack of a comprehensive strategy further compounded the issue.

Above: The railway companies took their responsibilities seriously in the 1930s. This group of London, Midland & Scottish Railway trainee mechanics are learning their trade with L plates tied round their waists.

Main: All manner of goods were transported by rail. Here an MG sports car is unloaded from a goods wagon at Addison Road Station for display at London's Olympia Motor Show in October 1932.

*Main: The future of steam still burned brightly when this London & North Eastern Railway
(LNER) class B1 No 61251 'Oliver Bury' left St Pancras Station, London, in June 1942.*

By the advent of World War II, the railway network
was still crucial in the movement of troops and other
personnel, however, it was only a matter of time before
further changes were imminent. Between 1939 and 1945
the rail network proved vital, once again, but a greatly
neglected system – facing stiff transport competition and
further developments in technology – saw the railways
nationalized in 1948. The next 50 years would provide a
checkered history, see the demise of steam and bring in
controversial privatization. The railway revolution and a
new way to travel had, sadly, come to an end.

SCAN WITH
layar
See page 5
for instructions

*Above: The East Coast mainline and its centres of engineering like York were prime
targets for the German Air Force between 1940 and 1943. In this image, the 'Sir
Ralph Wedgwood' A4 class 4-6-2 steam locomotive No 4469 lies damaged in the
wreckage of York North locomotive depot, following an air raid on 29 April 1942.*

Famous Locomotives

Just how complex and sophisticated the steam
engine ultimately became can be indicated
by a selection of some of the most famous
locomotives in the history of British Steam.

Stirling Single

Patrick Stirling arrived at Great Northern Railway
in the latter half of the 19th Century, charged with
organizing the company's rolling stock. The railway
company had no standard rolling stock and Stirling first
set about designing a locomotive capable of handling his
ideas for improvements. He based his "single-wheeler"
design on a locomotive at Great Eastern Railway, which
resulted in two designs by 1868. These both comprised a
2-2-2 wheel arrangement with seven foot, one inch driving
wheels. However, this was extended, and two years later,
Stirling had designed driving wheels of 8 foot 1 inch, for
a locomotive capable of "high" speeds for GNR traffic
between London and York. Due to the large drivers,
Stirling set his cylinders outside with a four-wheeled bogie
for stability.

The 53 locomotives were built at Doncaster over a period
of 25 years and produced in three series in 1870, 1884 and
1894 and numbered out of sequence by GNR. The 'Stirling
Single'   No 1 class were designed for passenger rolling
stock – of up to 26 carriages – and nicknamed the
"Eight Footer".

*Main: 'Stirling Single' 4-2-2 steam locomotive No 1 was a
successful design that ran for 30 years.*

Managing an average speed of around 50 mph, the 'Stirling Single' entered the Race to the North in 1895. The Race to the North took place in the summer of 1888 and 1895 when railway companies raced each other from north London to Scotland over two trunk routes via the West Coast mainline (from Euston in London, via Crewe and Carlisle), and the East Coast mainline which travelled from King's Cross through York and Newcastle. (Patrick Stirling's GNR Stirling No 775 made the East Coast route between Grantham and York – a total of 92 miles – in one hour and 16 minutes.) However, it was a hotly contested race, which often left passengers rather disconcerted (it was a largely bumpy ride) and the racing was abandoned in favour of more safety and comfort. The 'Stirling Single' No 1 class is the only one of its kind that was preserved and today it can be found in the National Railway Museum in York.

Main: The 4-6-2 locomotive number 4472 'Flying Scotsman' pictured as presented at the British Empire Exhibition in 1924.

Above: The large drive wheel gave the 'Stirling Single' a distinctive look.

SCAN WITH
layar
See page 5
for instructions

Flying Scotsman

Built in Doncaster at a cost of £7,945, one of the most famous locomotives of them all, the 'Flying Scotsman' was the flagship engine of the London & North Eastern Railway (LNER). It was designed to travel a journey of 390 miles between Edinburgh and King's Cross in London in the early 1900s. When it was showcased in February 1923 it was known as the 'Special Scotch Express' and arrived in time for the Railway Groupings Act 1924, when LNER became part of the "Big Four". It was a powerful marketing tool for the railway company, which helped LNER establish itself as a major player on the railway network despite the Great Depression of the 1930s. It was particularly impressive for its speed.

Above: First class dining car interior on the 1909 'Flying Scotsman'.

Journey times were cut by more than three hours, to around seven and a half hours, and passengers could enjoy luxuries including fine cuisine, a cocktail bar and even hairdressing facilities. It led to an illustrious history of service for the Class A3 Pacific locomotive No 4472 (originally No 1472), which was to last 80 years. Its performance and the facilities it offered in its carriages were so popular that it inspired a film, "The Flying Scotsman" in 1929, just one year after the 'Special Scotch Express' was renamed. Mechanical improvements had been implemented in 1924 when chief mechanical engineer Sir Nigel Gresley ensured that the locomotive could run non-stop, with one tender of coal, between London and the Scottish capital. This feat led to the 'Flying Scotsman' setting the world record as the first steam locomotive to officially reach 100 miles per hour in November 1934.

During the Second World War, the locomotive found itself as a vital part of the war effort when it was commissioned to move freight, as well as military and civilian traffic.

When the 'Flying Scotsman' was "retired" following the recommendations to dramatically reduce the railway network by Dr Richard Beeching, it was headed for the breaker's yard in the mid-1950s. However, it was Eastern Regional Board member for British Railways Alan Pegler who negotiated that the locomotive could remain on the East Coast mainline as a nostalgic reminder of the glory of steam. Following the purchase, and a tour of the United Sates, the 'Flying Scotsman' was bought by William McAlpine. A second tour resulted in a further record when the 'Flying Scotsman' toured Australia in August 1989 and recorded the longest non-stop run by a steam locomotive of 422 miles.

The most famous passenger locomotive in history was bought for the nation in 2004 and is housed at the National Railway Museum in York.

Above: 'Flying Scotsman' at rest.

Main: The A4 class 4-6-2 locomotive number 60022 'Mallard', designed by Sir Nigel Gresley and built at Doncaster Works.

'Mallard' is officially the fastest steam locomotive in the world.

Mallard

'Mallard' set a new world steam speed record on 3 July 1938 when it reached a staggering speed of 126 mph. Designed by Sir Nigel Gresley, the 4-6-2 Class A4 (No 4468), like the 'Flying Scotsman', was built in Doncaster and destined for the East Coast mainline. Chief mechanical engineer Gresley built the locomotive at a cost of £8,500 during the early 1930s and was inspired to name the engine after the mallards he had fed during some leisure time, away from the workshops. Gresley had been under increasing pressure to design faster, reliable locomotives during the years of the Great Depression, when road transport was considered a serious threat to the profitability of the railway. He designed a more streamlined A3 model locomotive that was taken from the drawing board to the workshops, but competition from trains across the globe was fast gaining on British engineers and pressure was tough.

Main: The 100th Pacific Class engine to be built, in November 1937, was named after its designer, Sir Nigel Gresley, who holds a silver model of his creation (centre).

Above: Foot plate of 'Mallard'. Seen to the upper left of the fire hole is the steam chest pressure gauge, while to the right is the boiler pressure gauge.

Above: The A4 Great Reunion at the National Railway Museum in July 2008: 'Bittern', 'Sir Nigel Gresley' and 'Union of South Africa' with the world record-holding 'Mallard'.

It was down to Gresley to design something far more unique than he had first envisaged with the reliable and solid A3 model. Following wind tunnel testing, the A4 class was designed with phenomenal streamlining. Improvements included a new super-powered steam locomotive for journeys from King's Cross in London to Newcastle upon Tyne in the North East which began in 1935. (The locomotive made its inaugural journey between the north London station and Grantham in the East Midlands in September 1935. After the crew managed an impressive speed of 112 mph, the chief mechanical engineer advised them to slow the train.) Speed was of the essence for 'Mallard' and three further A4 locomotives joined it on one of the network's busiest routes, which managed to cut the journey time to four hours. It was an impressive feat by a pioneering Gresley, who had found his original designs for 'Mallard' under scrutiny. The route was popular with passengers and, as demand grew for alternatives, services were rolled out to Leeds and Bradford and the first inter-city network began to take shape.

With increasing pressure on LNER for locomotive design, not just from overseas companies but the three other members of the "Big Four", 'Mallard' was chosen as the locomotive that would set a new world record for speed. On a planned brake testing trial, the locomotive set out from Grantham on the journey back to London and Gresley recorded a speed of 126 mph before the locomotive was steadied to around 120 mph. While the locomotive had to undergo some repairs after overheating, 'Mallard' had proved that it was a force to be reckoned with on the railway network and a plaque was attached to the foot plate, following official recognition for the record. 'Mallard' is on display at the National Railway Museum in York.

Golden Arrow

Southern Railway (SR) unveiled their luxury boat train 'Golden Arrow' in 1926. Also known as 'Flèche d'Or' (on the French side of the Channel), the service was pivotal in the passenger traffic which linked London with the port of Dover on the Kent coast. As passengers alighted from the carriages, they were met by the ferry, which would transport them to Calais in France, before making an onward journey to Paris. Passengers enjoyed a first class Pullman service once they reached Calais, but this was extended to include the London to Dover route some three years later in May 1929. The locomotive – more often than not a Lord Nelson class – pulled 10 British Pullman cars for the 98-minute journey from London, but faced stiff competition from air travel and both locomotives and first-class ferries were forced to include lower-fee-paying travellers, especially with the advent of the Great Depression in the 1930s. Following the Second World War, passenger services were resumed in April 1946 with a bar and a pre-war Pullman, but these were later upgraded and replaced by the start of the following decade in order to play their part in the 1951 Festival of Britain.

Today, the Bluebell Railway in Sussex still runs a 'Golden Arrow' service.

Main: 'Golden Arrow' cross Channel boat train service leaving Shakespeare Cliff tunnel at Dover in 1948.

Main: Staff standing in front of the Pullman carriages of the
'Fleche D'Or', also known as the 'Golden Arrow', in October 1947.

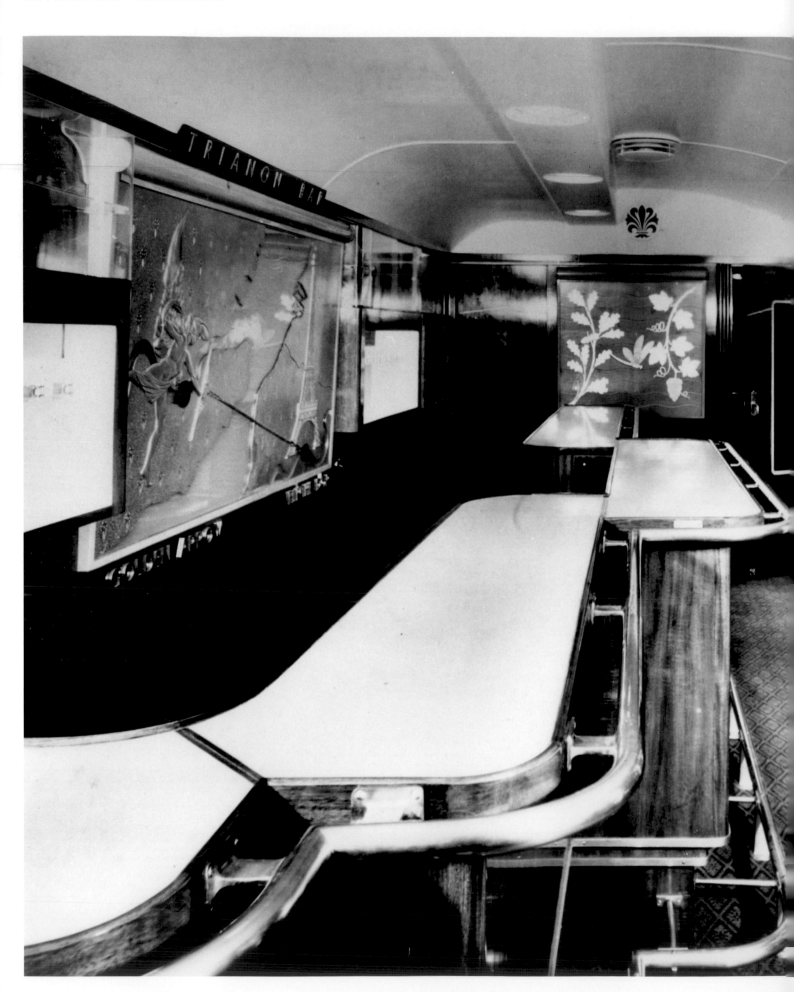

*Above: The entrance for Golden Arrow
passengers at Victoria Station, circa 1935.*

*Main: Interior of the Trianon Bar in the Pullman Buffet Car No
5, which operated on the prestigious Golden Arrow boat train
service between London's Victoria Station and Dover.*

City of Truro

The 'City of Truro', No 3717 (originally No 3440 between 1903 and 1912), was the first steam locomotive to reach a speed of more than 100 mph. The City class, designed by George Jackson, in Swindon, unofficially reached 102 mph in May 1904. From its first days in service, the locomotive was renowned for its performance, particularly its speed but, with only one timekeeper on the foot plate and speculation about the capabilities of the 'City of Truro', the record remained unrecognized. The locomotive was designed to reach a speed of up to 85 mph, although timekeeper and journalist for "Railway Magazine" Charles Rous-Marten was adamant that the engine had reached 102 mph on the steep decline from Whiteball, on the 128-mile journey from Plymouth to Pylle Hill Junction in Bristol. Certainly, his detailed account and timekeeping do indicate that the locomotive could have achieved this speed, however, doubters were sceptical that the small 4-4-0-class, pulling mail freight, could have managed such a speed. Rumors also abounded that even if the 'City of Truro' had reached more than 100 mph, it was as a result of bad judgment by the driver, a man called Clements. Over the years, many have tried to calculate how fast the locomotive may have travelled, and a number of experts theorise that the likely maximum speed, bearing in mind the ihp of the engine and the 148 tons it was pulling, would equate to around 90 mph. Inaccurate claims with regard to speed were fairly common, but this Great Western Railway locomotive certainly caused a huge controversy at the time.

The 'City of Truro' was later replaced by more substantial locomotives, but returned to service in 1957 on the Newbury to Southampton branch line. It was "retired" in 1961 and is housed in the National Railway Museum in York.

Main: The restored 'City of Truro' hauling a special excursion train on the York-Scarborough line in 1996.

Tornado

British Railways built 49 locomotives in the Peppercorn A1 series between 1948 and 1949, although they were originally ordered by LNER. They were designed to provide services for heavy traffic following the Second World War. However, after just 14 years, the series was scrapped completely. In 1990, the A1 Trust was formed and decided to build 'Tornado' from scratch as an evolution of the Peppercorn class, as it may have been had steam not suffered a demise. 'Tornado', No 60103, like the original Peppercorn A1 series, was built at Darlington and completed in 2008.

Named after the Panavia Tornado combat aircraft, construction got underway in 1994 following fund raising activities, donations and sponsorships. Full certification was granted in 2009 and 'Tornado' is now employed on heritage railways and passenger services on the rail network and housed at Crewe Heritage Centre.

'Tornado' was the first steam train to be built in Britain for almost 50 years.

Above: Enthusiasts celebrate Britain's first steam engine in almost 50 years.

Main: The new Peppercorn Class A1 steam locomotive 'Tornado' arriving at
York railway station for its naming ceremony in February 2009.

Duchess of Hamilton

The Princess Coronation class locomotives were built as powerful express passenger engines for the London, Midland & Scottish Railway (LMS) on the West Coast mainline. The 'Duchess of Hamilton', No 6229, was the tenth of the class to built in Crewe in 1938, designed by William Stanier. The locomotive, which comprised streamline casing, was a sleek modern locomotive that spent its first year in New York in the United States as a prominent example of pioneering British engineering.

The 'Duchess of Hamilton', along with other locomotives of her class was renowned for her speed and reliability. While it remains questionable whether the streamlined casing around the boiler did improve performance, there was no doubting that renowned engineer Stanier had enhanced the Princess Royal Class on which the locomotive was based. As one of the second batch of five locomotives built, the 'Duchess of Hamilton' was painted red (alongside the 'Duchess of Gloucester', the 'Duchess of Norfolk', the 'Duchess of Devonshire' and the 'Duchess of Rutland') to match new rolling stock, rather than the Caledonian Railway blue that had graced the five earlier engines. These included the 'Coronation', the 'Queen Elizabeth', the 'Queen Mary', the 'Princess Alice' and the 'Princess Alexandra'.

Main: 'Duchess of Hamilton' 4-6-2 Class 8P steam locomotive and tender, designed by Sir William Stanier for London, Midland & Scottish Railway in 1938.

When it was proved in 1946 that the casing did little to enhance performance, particularly at slower speeds, following the recommendations of mechanical staff, the casing was removed and by 1949 all traces of the "bullet" were removed. Newer locomotives in the class included the 'Duchess of Atholl', the 'Duchess of Montrose', the 'Duchess of Sutherland' and the 'Duchess of Abercorn'.

When retired, the 'Duchess of Hamilton' was saved from the breaker's yard at Barry in South Wales by Billy Butlin, who installed the locomotive as a playground attraction at a holiday camp. It was later sent on a long term, 20-year loan to the National Railway Museum in York, before it was purchased for permanent preservation in 1987. In 2007, the 'Duchess of Hamilton' was unveiled once again with a replica rebuild of her streamlined casing to celebrate the 70th anniversary of the Coronation Scot service for which she was built.

Above: A streamlined 'Duchess of Hamilton' in the 21st Century.

Above: Restoration is carried out in the 1980s.

Main: The unveiling ceremony of 'Evening Star', class
9F 2-10-0 locomotive number 92220, in April 1960.

Evening Star

The 'Evening Star' was built in Swindon as a class 9F locomotive for express freight with its five coupled driving wheels designed for the purpose. It was unveiled in the spring of 1960 and holds the honour of being the last steam locomotive built in Britain when steam was still a way of life. The class 2-10-0, No 92220, had a two-wheeled leading wagon with 10 driving wheels and was capable of pulling extremely large and heavy freight.

'Evening Star's name was chosen following a competition to recognise what was known to be the last steam locomotive to leave the Swindon workshops. It was the only one of its class to be given a name, which aptly reflected that it signified the end of an era. (One of the earliest locomotives had been appropriately named 'Morning Star'.) All other locomotives in its class were painted black as heavy haulage freight engines, however, 'Evening Star' was painted in livery green while its double chimney was copper-capped. Built for British Railways (later renamed British Rail), the highly powered 9F locomotive was based at Cardiff in South Wales where, despite being a freight engine, it was often used to transport the Red Dragon passenger express to London.

Towards the end of its working life, 'Evening Star' was transferred to the Somerset & Dorset Railway, where it was pivotal in hauling passenger carriages and freight wagons before the line was finally closed and the locomotive was retired in 1965. While it had been designed to last a further 20 years, the recommendations of the Beeching report saw the end of an era before its time. Today, 'Evening Star' is one of nine preserved 9F locomotives and is housed at the National Railway Museum in York.

Princess Margaret Rose

The 'Princess Margaret Rose', No 46203 (originally No 6203), was built in Crewe in 1935 and was designated as the Princess Royal Class. Named after the five-year-old daughter of the Duke (who became King George VI in December 1936) and Duchess of York, the locomotive was the third in her class to be built as an express passenger engine.

Stanier began as an apprentice under William Dean for Great Western Railways in his native hometown, Swindon. He was promoted to principal assistant to the company's chief mechanical engineer before moving to the London, Midland & Scottish Railways (LMS) in 1932, where he was enticed by Josiah Stamp. He arrived as chief mechanical engineer to turn around the company's fortunes, at that time dogged by in-fighting amongst the staff from former railway companies that had merged under the Groupings Act some eight years earlier. Despite intense competition from the three other members of the "Big Four", LMS had very few heavy express passenger or freight locomotives and Stanier (who was knighted for his services to engineering in 1944) set about redressing the balance.

His work for LMS was exceptional – with the introduction of the Royal Class, the Princess Royal Class, and mixed traffic or "Black Five" locomotives, the Coronation Class and Jubilee mixed traffic locomotives. During Stanier's time, between 1932 and 1947, more than 2,000 of the world's most powerful steam locomotives were designed and built at LMS.

Main: 'Princess Margaret Rose', steam locomotive No 6203, on the West Coast mainline, Lune Gorge, Westmoreland (now Cumbria) in July 1936.

The 'Princess Margaret Rose' with a 4-6-2 wheel arrangement was designed and built specifically to transport the Royal Scot train running between Euston station in London and Glasgow. The Princess Royal Class employed steam turbines rather than the earlier cylinders and were known as "Lizzies" after Princess Elizabeth, Princess Margaret Rose's older sister. The 7P class was changed to an 8P in 1951 and included 12 locomotives in total, comprising the 'Princess Elizabeth', the 'Princess Margaret Rose', the 'Princess Royal', 'Princess Louise', 'Princess Victoria', 'Princess Marie Louise', 'Princess Beatrice', the 'Duchess of Kent', 'Princess Arthur of Connaught', 'Lady Patricia', 'Queen Maud' and 'Princess Helana Victoria'. 'Princess Margaret Rose' was retired in 1961 and saved from the breaker's yard by holiday camp owner Billy Butlin, who restored the locomotive and installed it at Gwynedd in 1963. The locomotive moved to the Midland Railway Centre, Derbyshire, in 1975 before being sold to the Princess Royal Locomotive Trust in 1985. The locomotive remains at the railway centre as a historic reminder of the huge developments made in steam engineering during the 1930s.

Above: Driver of the 'Princess Royal' class 4-6-2 locomotive number 6204 'Princess Louise' with a young boy and model train in 1938.

*Main: Railway workers lower the boiler into the frame of
the first London, Midland & Scottish Railway 4-6-2 steam
locomotive No 6200, 'Princess Royal', in 1933.*

Main: The GWR 6000 Class No 6024
King Edward I, 2 July 1930.

King Edward I

Chief Mechanical Engineer for Great Western Railway (GWR), Jackson Churchward, designed and built the 'King Edward I', No 6024, with its 4-6-0 wheel arrangement for the King class four cylinder engine in 1930. The class was arguably one of the most technologically advanced and superior on the rail network during the early 20th Century. Churchward was an innovative engineer, renowned for his designs, but the King class came into its own under the direction of his predecessor, Charles Collett, who oversaw the workshops in Swindon where the 'King Edward I' was built.

The locomotive was first based in Plymouth, before spending some of its working life based in the depot at Paddington in London. It was one of the largest, most efficient locomotives of its time and eventually moved to Cardiff Canton in shed 86C, where its previously unseen dimensions enabled it to perform efficiently and significantly at GWR's main engineering base. Weighing around 136 tons, 'King Edward I' was one of 30 of its class built between 1927 to 1930, and was produced in a second batch of 10. It cost around £7,500 to build and found its main run on the Paddington to the South West of England passenger express route until 1948.

As a result of its solid build, the locomotive clocked up an impressive mileage of more than one million miles by 1953 and was equipped with a superheated boiler, which enabled speeds in excess of 90 mph. The reliable King class locomotives became renowned for their ability to match the British Railways timetabling after nationalization in January 1948 and this led to the domination of the class as heavy haulers until the demise of steam and the advent of diesel engines. In fact, the 'King Edward I' had proved so robust that it continued in mainline services right up until all King class locomotives were removed from service in 1962.

Once it was retired, the 'King Edward I' was sent to the breaker's yard, owned by the Woodham Brothers, in Barry, South Wales where it remained for a number of years before preservation began. It was bought in 1973 by the King Preservation Society and housed at the Buckinghamshire Railway Centre. Restoration took the Society more than 16 years, but in 1989, the 'King Edward I' was once more on the tracks.

Right: 'Green Arrow' was built at Doncaster in 1936 and withdrawn from service in 1962.

Below: A BR poster advertising the Green Arrow Service, circa 1955.

Green Arrow

Sir Nigel Gresley was responsible for locomotive No 4771, named the 'Green Arrow' – built for the London & North Eastern Railway (LNER) in 1936. It was a V2 steam locomotive designed for mixed traffic but took its name from one of the freight services it operated. The 'Green Arrow' was the first of its class to be built (in Doncaster) and was based on the class A1 and A2 Pacifics. Its smaller driving wheels, with their 2-6-2 arrangement, however, enabled its design to incorporate a three-cylinder arrangement, favoured by LNER's chief mechanical engineer. It was the specific wheel arrangement, requiring a large firebox, which meant that the 'Green Arrow' was one of the first major locomotives of any class of its type.

One hundred and eighty four V2 class were built, in batches, between 1936 and 1944, and were the only locomotives to be built during the Second World War.

This was as a result of the value of these locomotives, which had more than proved their worth prior to the outbreak of war in 1939. However, of these locomotives, just eight were named, including the 'Green Arrow'. The other seven locomotives consisted of the 'Green Howard', 'Durham School', 'King's Own Yorkshire Light Infantry', the 'Snapper', 'St Peter's School York', the 'Durham Light Infantry' and the 'Cold streamer', and proved to be useful for high-profile mixed traffic, which propelled Gresley to national recognition.

In 1933, Gresley's design incorporated the 2-6-2 arrangement leading to his preferred large firebox. It was based on the previous K3 2-6-0 wheel arrangement and streamlined further by 1934 (with the cab based on the smaller A4 class). The V2 class was a resounding success when unveiled in 1936 and the 'Green Arrow' was routed between King's Cross in London and journeyed north towards Glasgow on the East Coast mainline.

Despite their reliability on the railway network, the V2 pony trucks were less dependable and several derailments led to the introduction of replacement trucks prior to 1947. For the next 15 years, the V2 class continued unabated until they were withdrawn from service in the early 1960s. The 'Green Arrow' is now on display as part of the National Railway Collection at the National Railway Museum in York.

Main: 'U1 Garratt' is shown to members of
the press and public in July 1925.

U1 Garratt

Designed by Sir Henry Fowler, the U1 Class was responsible for working operations on the route between South Yorkshire coal mines from West Silkstone Junction to Wentworth Junction. Built in 1925, by Beyer Peacock, the 'U1 Garratt', No 2395, was charged with a steeply graded line with, at one point, a gradient of about one in 40 over three and a half miles. There were three cylinders per engine which was based on the LNER Q4 class and modified by Sir Nigel Gresley before it left the workshops.

The locomotive was unveiled at the Stockton & Darlington centenary celebrations in July 1925 and began service less than a month later. It was meant to be one of two locomotives of its kind, but only the 'U1 Garratt' was ever built to Fowler's design. It was nicknamed the 'Wath Banker', as a result of its services which included spending much of its time waiting for locomotives transporting coal to arrive from Wath. It was then manoeuvred from the siding at Worsborough Bank to be coupled with the arriving locomotive. From here, the 'U1 Garratt' would double-head the haul to the Silkstone Junction. However, the locomotive suffered a number of setbacks when it was found to be unreliable.

By 1930, the locomotive was out of service for around 12 months – due to mechanical problems – and in 1946, was renumbered No 9999, before a further renumber saw it labelled as locomotive No 69999 in the nationalization of the railways under British Railways, in January 1948. 'U1 Garratt' was transferred to the Lickey Incline just prior to the start of the 1950s, but was scrapped in 1955.

*Main: Early steam engines (circa 1816) – Watt's improved steam engine,
figs 119-122, and Hornblower's steam engine, figs 123-125.*

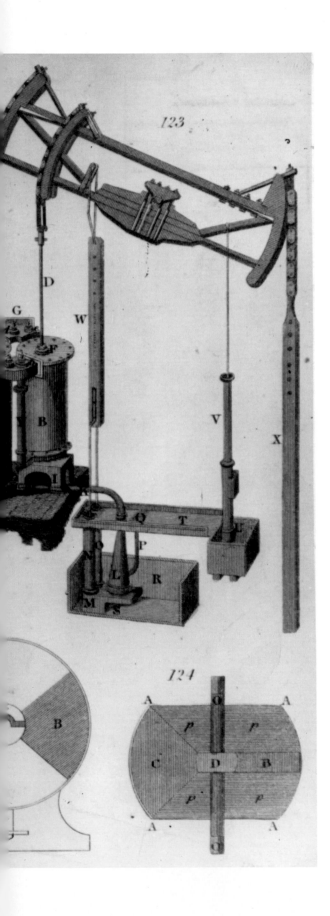

How It Works

The steam engine is an external combustion engine (as distinct, for instance, from a diesel locomotive or a motor car, which have internal combustion engines): steam as the working 'fluid' is kept separate from the heat source, and the combustible products. In fact, on early steam locomotives, this separation is very clear: the 'firebox' (the heat source) occupies a place quite distinct from that of the boiler (and indeed the fuel source itself - the coal usually being stored in a separate wagon or 'tender'). A steam engine employs a heat source of some type to boil water, which then turns into steam, and it is the expansion pressure of this steam which is then used to move pistons, or turbines, or otherwise generate motion.

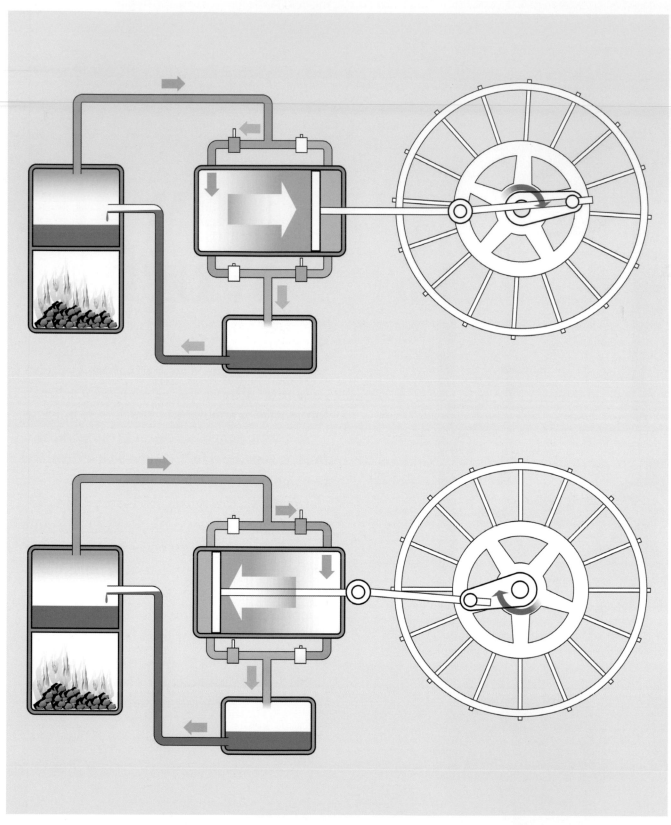

Above: Digital illustration of coal burning in a firebox producing heat which transfers to boiling water, then saturated steam, which in turn powers a piston forwards and backwards to drive a wheel.

Above: Escaping bubbles of steam in boiling water. Pure water boils at 100 degrees Celsius at the standard atmospheric pressure of 101325 pascals.

The term "steam engine" can cause some confusion at times because while it is often used to refer to a mechanism or machine in its entirety – such as a steam locomotive (thus embracing all parts of the locomotive from the boiler to the valve gear and wheels) – the words "steam engine" can also refer quite specifically just to the piston, or to the turbine – in other words, the epicentre where motion is initiated by the steam (the "motor unit"). In either scenario, mechanical work is performed by applying methods of alternately heating and cooling steam, in order to vary pressure. Importantly, the practical development of the steam engine greatly helped our understanding of thermodynamic theory, and certainly James Watt appreciated, for example, how the boiling point of water changed with pressure.

The latent energy contained within water is released once it reaches its boiling point of 100 degrees Celsius at normal atmospheric pressure. But in an enclosed vessel, where the steam cannot escape while heat continues to be applied, huge pressures can be built up by the compressed steam. (Indeed, high pressure locomotives were once called "strong steam" engines.) When steam is released in a controlled way, the force of the elastic and expanding steam can be directed to perform mechanical work – most usually by admitting the steam into one or more tubes containing metal plungers (in other words, setting in motion pistons that can then move to and fro in their cylinders).

Before Thomas Newcomen's time, steam engine technology was in its infancy.

The basic components of a steam engine, and the physical properties of steam, were undoubtedly known to, and explored by, the Ancient Greeks. From their writings, we know that they understood about atmospheric pressure, about vacuums, and how motion and sound might be generated by forcing steam through tubes and other restricted spaces. By the 17th Century (and possibly much earlier), it was realized that quickly cooling a vessel containing steam would initiate a rapid collapse of pressure as the steam condensed back into water, and various theories began to emerge as to how this phenomenon might be turned to practical use.

The principles (and indeed the machinery) involved in Thomas Newcomen's first practical working steam engine were, in fact, very simple. His key insight was to manufacture and employ that breakthrough component demonstrated by Denis Papin – the piston – and to make a connection in his mind between the concept of using steam pressure in order to lift a piston with the idea of then rapidly cooling it (so causing a contraction), and then to continue this cycle repeatedly, so that expansion and contraction initiated an up-down motion of the piston. While Newcomen was soon able to fashion a tube with a sufficiently tight seal to work such a useful piston, it was James Watt who really perfected the piston seal. Steam-driven pistons were thus much more efficient by the end of the 18th Century than they were at the start of that century; indeed, the first beam engines had a comparatively high wastage of steam, fuel and power.

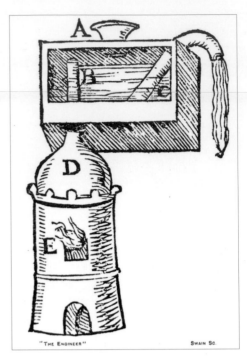

Above: An early steam engine from 1589 causing a ball to revolve on a pivot over a heated cauldron of water (inspired by an Ancient Greek 'aeolipile').

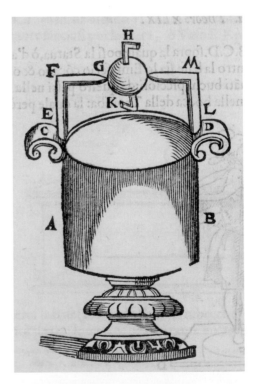

Above: Illustrated plate taken from 'De spiritali' (1606) by Italian scientist Giambattista Della Porta (1535-1615), showing a steam engine.

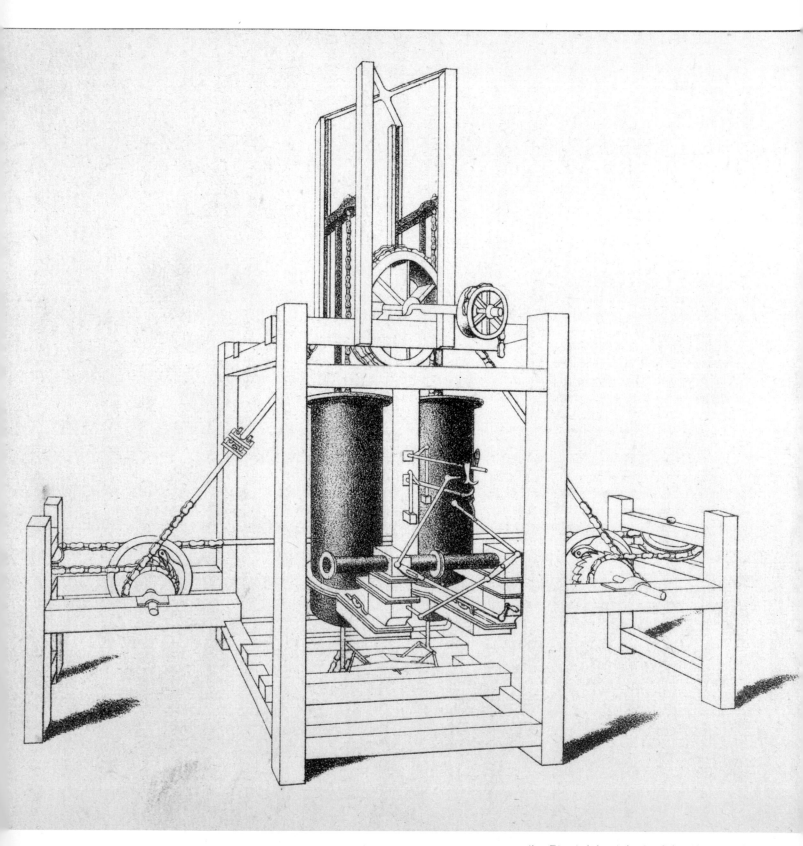

Above: This engine had two single-action cylinders, with separate condensers, which drove two paddle shafts by chains and ratchets, and was used in the first experimental steamboat, built by Patrick Miller (1731-1815) in 1788.

Newcomen's engines relied upon the injection of steam at atmospheric pressure into a cylinder, which then pushed up a vertical piston. By linking this piston by a chain to a counterweighted beam (which rocked on a central pivot point), it would force down a rod – usually into a mine shaft. Next, the steam that filled the cylinder, and which had pushed the piston to the top of its stroke, was condensed and this began to pull a vacuum. The vacuum in the cylinder, coupled with the atmospheric pressure acting on the top of the cylinder, would begin to drive the piston in the opposite direction – downwards – so pulling up the rod on the other side of the beam. In very basic terms, the elements required to create the first practical working steam engine were: the generation of steam in a rudimentary boiler, a piston and cylinder, a counterweighted beam, and the utilisation of normal air pressure working against that same steam, now condensed.

It was, of course, a little more complex than that, as there needed also to be various tubes, valves, linkages and a water reservoir. At the bottom of the cylinder a steam inlet valve opened and closed as the machine rocked (being linked to a thin parallel rod on a pivoting joint) and another tube led down from a cistern into the bottom of the cylinder, which squirted in cold water as the piston rose in order to condense the steam. Yet another parallel rod hanging from the beam worked an auxiliary pump so that the cistern could be kept topped up with water. The boiler sat directly under the piston in Newcomen's 1712 engine, and the fire was lit beneath that.

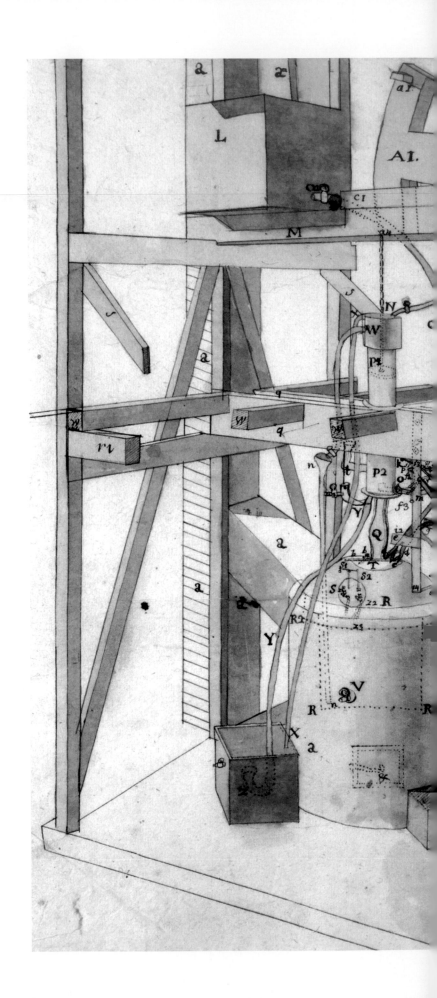

Above: Newcomen's atmospheric engine, circa 1730.

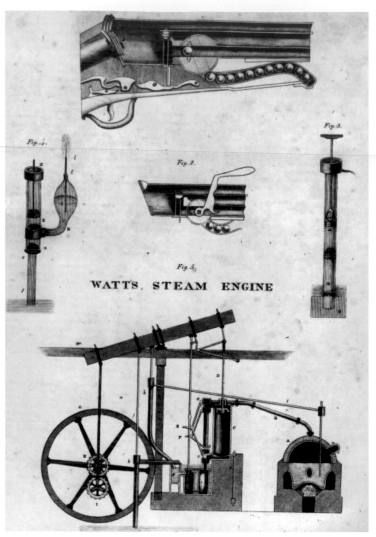

Above: Diagrams of pistons and valves, and James Watt's steam engine, circa 1785.

Above: Until 1800 the weakness of existing boilers had restricted most engines to being atmospheric ones. Trevithick set about making a cylindrical boiler which could withstand steam at higher pressures.

One of James Watt's first main improvements to Newcomen's engine involved him sealing off the upper part of the piston cylinder, which had previously been open – thereafter also enabling low pressure steam to be admitted through another opening in the top of the cylinder, rather than merely relying on atmospheric pressure to drive down the top of the piston. This low pressure steam exerted a greater force than atmospheric pressure, thus increasing power on the downward stroke.

An entire steam engine or steam plant might be said to consist, in very basic terms, of two overall components: a boiler (or steam generator) and a "motor unit". But the essential task in constructing any useful engine was, of course, in the first instance to be able to generate steam.

The Boiler

A steam engine may be powered by one or more boilers. The first incarnation of the boiler in the 18th Century involved building a type of brick oven in which sat a closed tank, so that flames and smoke could pass underneath and around the boiler. Next came rather odd-looking (and unsafe) low-pressure "haystack" and "wagon"-type boilers, later followed by stronger "egg-ended" ones, which incorporated a fire grate. Richard Trevithick invented the "Cornish boiler", capable of working at higher pressures, about 1812 (although he first obtained a "high-pressure" engine patent ten years earlier, in 1802). This sturdy, large horizontal cylinder incorporated a furnace tube to distribute heat more evenly, and also to help brace the boiler. From then on, smaller and faster engines could be made that were more and more powerful in relation to their cylinder size, which was exactly what was required for transport applications.

Above: In order for steam locomotion to be viable, it was essential that boiler size be reduced in comparison to this steam boiler at the Clydestream boatworks.

Above: French engineer Marc Seguin (1786-1875).

Following the example of Stephenson's 'Rocket', hot gases that issued from the firebox were fed through what evolved into a series of fire tubes running throughout the boiler, allowing for more thorough heating over a greater surface area. (This idea may not originally have been George Stephenson's, for he possibly learned the concept of the firebox "fire tube boiler" from the distinguished French engineer Marc Seguin, around 1827; nevertheless, inspiration flowed both ways, because Seguin had initially been inspired in his work by seeing Stephenson's 'Locomotion' in operation, in 1825.)

In the early years of the 19th Century, solutions began to appear to the great problem that had previously prevented engines from becoming mobile, and so develop into "locomotives": both boilers and their associated component engine parts were very large and heavy. Even as they became lighter and more compact, early engines still regularly broke tracks, not only due to the weight of the contraptions themselves sitting upon them, but also because the engines often had vertical cylinders that exerted a huge pressure on the relatively fragile rails with each downward stroke of the piston. Stronger rails and horizontal pistons were part of a larger solution that ultimately assisted in making rail travel more viable.

Above: Perspective view of 'Rocket's' firebox taken from page 64 of the notebook belonging to John Urpeth Rastrick that was used to record details of the Rainhill locomotive trials in 1829.

It was appreciated early on that locomotives should be insulated or "lagged" to prevent heat loss. This was initially done by fitting wooden batons lengthways around the boiler, then holding the batons in place with a series of metal bands. In time, other lagging materials were used, and were themselves encased in sheet metal boiler "clothing" or "cleading".

Building up "a head of steam", or having a sufficient head of steam in the boiler – in other words, the pressure needed to make a locomotive start moving – was one of many terms that came into being with the steam age. Indeed, many other similar expressions emerged from, or were reinforced by, 19th-Century railway terminology. These included idioms such as: "full steam ahead", "letting off steam", being a "slow coach", "going off the rails" (or otherwise "off track"), getting "derailed", coming to the "end of the line", desiring to "fast track", to "railroad" or to "shunt aside" something, needing to "backtrack", being on the "right track" – or the "wrong track" – or coming from the "wrong side of the tracks", having a "one track mind" or "tunnel vision", "chugging along", "making the grade", and even being "just the ticket"!

Main: 'Full steam ahead' as this Manchester to St Pancras Express No 723 heads through Cromford Station in Derbyshire, in June 1911.

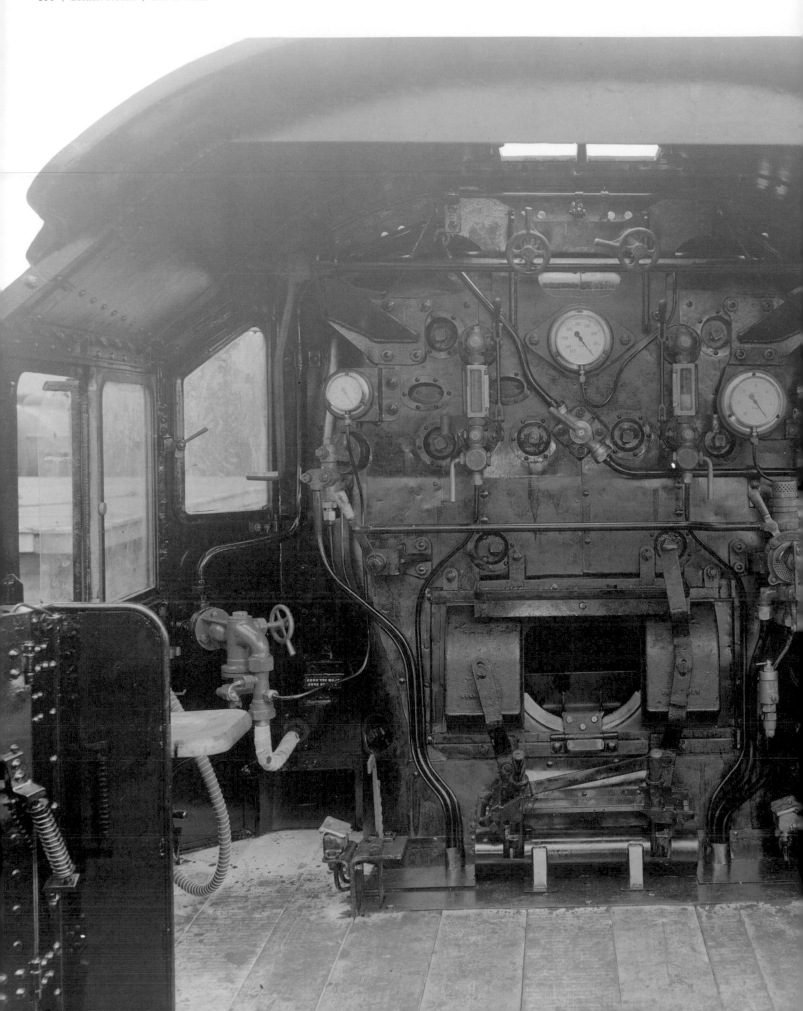

Boiler and Engine Fittings

Essential boiler fittings included "water gauges" to monitor the water level, "pressure gauges" to indicate steam pressure, "check valves" to control the boiler's supply of "feed water" (which was usually pumped in), "safety valves" to release excess steam (and so prevent calamity), and "junction valves" to regulate the steam leaving the boiler. Ultra-safe spring-loaded, tamper proof automatic safety valves had ultimately to be introduced to release pressure when it became too much for the boiler to work safely. These replaced early manual and other inefficient safety valves that were too prone to human error, accident or risk-taking. (The pressure gauge had a red warning line and, if pressure rose above it, the safety valve was meant to blow open at this point.) Another safety device located in the top of the locomotive firebox was a fusible plug, with lead at its centre, automatically set to melt whenever the water level in the boiler dropped and became too low. The remaining water and steam then ingeniously poured onto the fire, so aiming to extinguish it and thus prevent the boiler from overheating.

Main: The array of gauges and controls may look daunting to the uninitiated, but would be instantly familiar to the driver.

Above: Richard's steam engine indicator, 1862.

On his early rotary stationary steam engines, Watt had the insight to fit a "governor" – consisting of two spheres spinning on either side of a short arm, often made of brass – that acted by centrifugal force. As the governor rose up its spindle, it would tend to close a "throttle" valve and so slow the engine; while a falling governor would open the valve wider, speeding up the engine. The aim overall was to set an engine to work at a desired or optimum speed, and let the governor play a major role in maintaining that speed automatically. As early as 1851, Charles Richard developed another very helpful device, this time for analyzing the performance of a steam engine: the steam engine "indicator". The indicator graphically traced on paper the changes in pressure in a given cylinder throughout its entire cycle, and it proved so useful that it came to be used not only by engineers and mechanics but even by insurance inspectors in their quest to assess potential risks or detect actual problems. Horsepower could also be calculated quite accurately by using the steam engine indicator.

*Above: The high-pressure water tube boiler of the
W1 class 4-6-4 locomotive No 10,000, 1929.*

Left: Locomotive engines under construction in a workshop belonging to the Great Western Railway in April 1932.

Invented in the last decade of the 19th Century, the "superheater" was a device that directed the steam produced by the boiler through a tight and complex series of small tubes in the boiler flue, "drying" it out, in order to increase the temperature of the steam still further. This had the ultimate effect of making the pistons work more efficiently, saving up to 25% of the coal that might otherwise have been consumed. German engineer Wilhelm Schmidt is credited with the invention of the superheater around 1890, although it took until 1908 for a locomotive to use this device in Britain. Several GWR locos featured the superheater in the 20th Century, for which better steam cylinder oil had to be developed that was capable of withstanding the much higher temperatures generated. Another device, called an "economizer", which came into being much earlier in the 19th Century, followed the same principle as the superheater – in this case by pre-heating feed water before it entered the boiler, thus also saving on coal. Economizers became standard on 19th-century locomotives, for they reduced the "shock" of cold water entering a hot boiler, and so also helped with efficiency. Besides using steam from the boiler to drive the pistons, it came also to be used for many other auxiliary purposes – including activating whistles, pumps, brakes and even enabling passenger cars to be heated.

Tall chimneys on early locomotives gave way to "dampers" situated under the fire, which acted to force air through the burning coal and so facilitate combustion. (Both fire smoke and cylinder steam were exhausted through the boiler chimney – meeting first in a "smoke box", before being expelled.) When stationary for any length of time, firemen had to activate a "blower" so that sufficient draught was still flowing in, and by this means ensure that the fire was not extinguished.

Above: Early steam locomotives had a distinct 'dome' and a tall funnel.

ELLIOTT BROS 30 STRAND. LONDON.

Valves and Valve Gear

In the first practical steam engines, vertical cylinders dominated for many years, not least because it was thought that there would be severe wear with horizontal cylinders, especially due to the weight of early designs. But with appropriate and sufficient lubrication, this was later shown not, in fact, to be a serious problem. (However, for small locomotives working on very steep inclines, vertical boilers often remained the only practical option.)

Admission and exhaust from cylinders was controlled by valves that had to open and close at precisely the right time for optimum operation of the to-and-fro movement of the piston, and these valves were automated by being driven by the engine itself through various linkages (which ranged from being quite simple, to sometimes being very complicated). For each complete piston cycle in a reciprocating steam engine, the steam also reversed its stroke. Therefore, a full cycle consisted of two piston strokes and one revolution of the crank, and in addition, the following four events occurred: admission of the steam, then expansion, exhaust and compression.

Main: The locomotive shown in this model has a smoke box enclosing the cylinders. The valves were driven through a rocking shaft by four eccentrics and the ordinary link motion. A dome over the firebox carried a spring-loaded lever safety valve while another dome on the boiler barrel housed the regulator.

Above: This 700 hp horizontal cross compound mill engine with Corliss
valves, drove up to 1,500 weaving looms at the Finchley View Mill,
Harle Syke in Burnley in Lancashire, from 1903 to 1970.

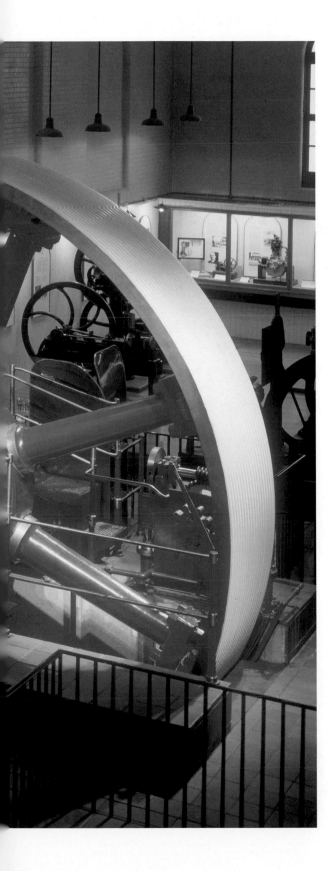

The valves that admitted and exhausted steam on the earliest engines – such as Newcomen's – were little more than manually-operated taps, but they gradually evolved into mechanically automated valve gear. By the 19th Century, most engines worked on the "double-acting" principle: which is to say that steam was admitted to each end of the cylinder alternately. For this to happen, taps – or more correctly – valves, had to be used. The earliest simple "plug"-type valves (which could stick) soon gave way to William Murdoch's more reliable "slide" valves, which moved across slots or "ports". (Murdoch worked for Boulton and Watt as their chief engine erector.) By contrast, Cornish engineers favoured improved, balanced, "double-beat drop valves" – being a pair of linked "plugs", where one was pushed down while the other pushed up.

In 1849, American engineer Henry Corliss (1817-88) made a major breakthrough with his "semi-rotary" or "rocking" valves, use of which became widespread throughout industry. Two of these Corliss valves were needed at the end of each cylinder. When moved by valve gear, Corliss valves twisted open and shut somewhat like a trap door. "Piston" valves (operating through openings into a small cylinder that ran parallel with the main steam cylinder) also came to be much used by the late 19th Century, because they needed relatively little effort to move them to and fro. Consequently, they were ideal for use on high speed locomotives.

SCAN WITH
layar
See page 5
for instructions

Above: Such was the impact of Boulton, Watt and Murdoch, that a statue of the trio was unveiled in Birmingham in 1956.

Above: Operating a steam locomotive underground presents its own problems as the restored 'Met Locomotive No. 1' – built in 1898 – demonstrates at Baker Street Station in December 2012.

Valve gear enabled both forward and reverse motion, and it was Stephenson's valve gear, or "link motion", of 1843 that predominated for many years on locomotives. (Stephenson's Link Motion was, in fact, the most commonly used valve gear on British industrial locomotives.) This device had the ability to alter whether steam was admitted to the front or back of the piston cylinder, when a "regulator" (effectively in this context a starting valve) was opened. The regulator was usually fitted in the "dome" of the boiler, and was used to control the flow of steam into the pistons – through a lever called a "regulator control", situated in the driver's cab. The steam from the boiler itself gathered, of course, along the whole

inside top of a locomotive boiler (in the "steam space"), and where – within the dome (the highest point) – there was a tube into which steam first entered as it embarked upon its journey towards the piston cylinders. The final release of exhaust steam out of the cylinders and up a "blastpipe" in the chimney is what causes a locomotive's characteristic "chuffing" sound. The blastpipe was quite an early invention that was needed to help increase draught through the fire. However, before being expelled, often condensed or reduced-pressure steam came to be used to power other secondary (or even tertiary) lower pressure cylinders in "compound" engines that had further "expansion" phases (so coming to be known as "double",

"triple", or even "quadruple expansion" engines). Unlike in most locomotives (which consumed large amounts of water), in marine and stationary engines, steam was increasingly recycled or fed back into the boiler in a "closed loop" in order to improve efficiency and reduce the need for constant refilling of water tanks. Certain steam locomotives, however – especially those working in arid conditions, and indeed several manufactured for use on the London Underground, where the atmosphere was very close – employed various ingenious devices to capture and re-condense some or most of the steam that was about to be exhausted. These were known as "closed cycle condensing steam engines".

The term "running gear" is an all-embracing one, as is also the similar blanket-term of "motion" – which refers in the latter case to all of the rods, links and levers (the connecting rods and valve gear) that comprise the "drive train" of the locomotive. "Running gear" actually refers to all the wheels and axles, and their associated items and supports (in other words, the wheel sets, axleboxes, brakes and springing – as well as the whole of the "motion").

In a steam locomotive, each piston transfers its power by means of a connecting rod and a crankpin, acting on the driving wheel, or on a crank on the axle. To help with traction, "sand boxes" were often fitted to help in situations where wheel adhesion was weak (in wet or icy conditions, for example). These allowed sand to run under the wheels, and were either worked by gravity, or assisted by steam or air injection.

*Main: Connecting rods and wheels on
No 92203 'Black Prince'.*

Above: Steam locomotives could be utilized to haul freight and/or passengers, like this Great Western Railway Pullman Express of 1870.

Chassis, Tender and Wheel Configurations

Locomotive wheels, sitting on their axles and anchored to the mainframe (or chassis), transmitted their effort to a "drawbar" at the rear, on which was fixed a hook, to which wagons were then attached by a suitable chain. The locomotive's frame supported the boiler and all the elements of the running gear. Locomotives needed more or less axles depending on the weight of the engine and the use to which the engine was put, for each axle had a maximum load that it could safely bear.

In broad terms, locomotives could be split into two types: tender and tank. Tank engines carried their water onboard in some variant of one or more tanks, as well as having an integrated coal bunker. They were compact and "self-contained". Tender locomotives, which were larger, had a quite separate wagon or tender (giving them longer range), in which was held all their required water and coal needs. (In 1825, the word "tender" was first applied to the engineers on locomotives, and the word stuck, referring initially to one who "tended" the engine; later, the term was depersonalized so that it came to represent just the wagon that tended the engine, and contained its essential supplies.)

Above: London, Midland & Scottish 0-4-0 locomotive No 10617 was built in 1911 at Horwich Works, Lancashire.

Above: A Craven 70-ton crane is shown lifting an 0 Class 0-4-4T locomotive at the North Eastern Railway's Darlington Works, circa 1902.

Above: South Eastern & Chatham Railway (SECR) 0-6-0 goods locomotive No 70 Class R was built at Ashford in June 1898 and withdrawn in January 1942.

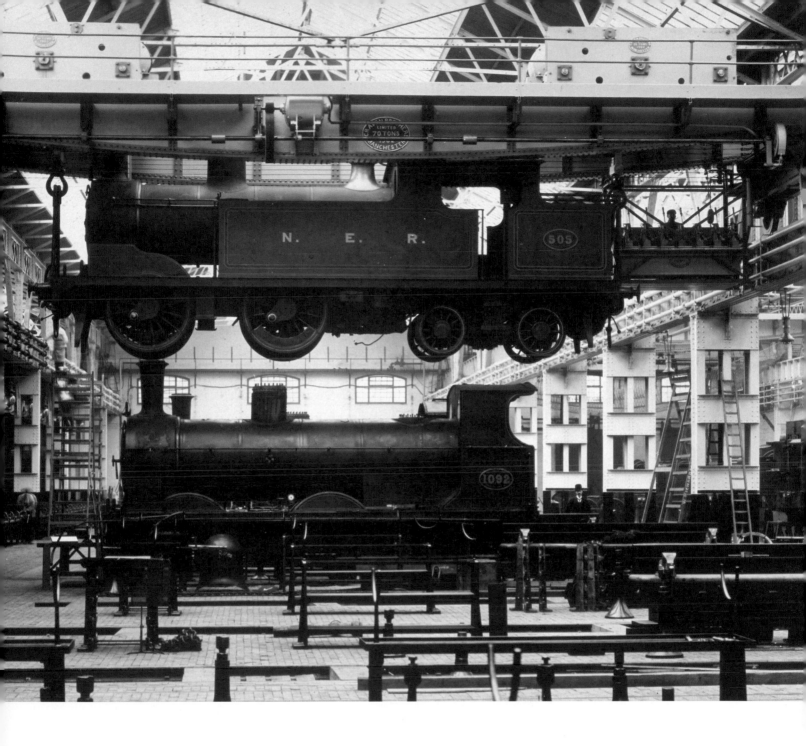

Frederick Methvan Whyte (1865-1941) was the originator of a system of "notation" that came to be employed in the early 20th Century in most English-speaking and Commonwealth countries in order to systematise and understand better locomotive wheel configurations. His system names three sets of wheels, in an order that defines the number of leading, driving and trailing wheels (each separated by a dash).

Wheel arrangements to some degree indicated what special use each type of locomotive had. The most common for industrial use were 0-4-0 and 0-6-0 locomotives. With their short wheelbase, for example, engines with an 0-4-0 configuration (two pairs of linked drive wheels) could easily pull goods around very tight curves, while larger 0-6-0 engines (with three pairs of linked drive wheels) were more powerful and stable, but couldn't be used on lines with very sharp curvature. (Long, rigid-wheelbase locomotives cannot travel around sharp curves unless they are articulated in some way. Whyte's notation dealt with articulated locomotives by using a "+" sign, as, for instance, with the 2-6-2+2-6-2 'Garratt'.)

Main: Midland Railway saddle tank
engine 0-6-0ST 1098A.

The different uses to which locomotives needed to be put – passenger and industrial – as well as the terrain and environments in which they worked, led to the creation of unique and distinct classes of locomotive (a shunter being quite different, in form and purpose, from a heavy goods or an express passenger locomotive, for example). Broad classes of larger locomotive often had a characteristic word as a suffix, stemming from the first use or initial type of the engine. When appended to Whyte notation, you would have, for example, a 4-6-2 'Pacific' Class locomotive. (Those with sufficient familiarity with steam locomotive types would instantly recognise from reading the wheel-configuration numbers 4-6-2 that the engine was likely to be a 'Pacific' Class tender locomotive, without being told so, and suitable for express passenger services – although there was also a 'Pacific' tank locomotive for hauling mineral traffic). The wheel configuration 4-6-2 meant it had a four-wheel leading bogie, six coupled driving wheels, and a two-wheel trailing bogie, or truck. The leading bogies on such express locomotives helped to provide stability at high speeds, while also acting as an initial guide for the locomotive as it entered a curve. Furthermore, some types of engines might also have a nickname, as with a 'Pug' engine (a type of 0-4-0 light shunting and industrial saddle tank locomotive, with a squashed-looking nose!). A single letter as suffix after the Whyte system also indicated a particular engine designation. For instance, the 'T' in 0-6-0T denoted a 'tank' (or 'side tank') engine, with other options including 'ST' for 'saddle tank', 'PT' for 'pannier tank', and 'WT' for 'well tank'. No suffix indicated a tender locomotive.

Above: Sir Nigel Gresley was knighted for his services to the railway industry in 1936.

Groupings and classifications became more sophisticated as the years progressed, and British Railways followed the practice of denoting locomotives according to their main use, using 'P' (passenger), 'F' (freight) and 'MT' (mixed traffic) – and then (from 1951) a power rating was also added for their primary and secondary roles (0-8 for passenger, 0-9 for freight, and 2-7 for mixed). Thus A4 Pacifics were rated '8P6F' – high up on the scale for passenger work, and reasonably high for freight. This designation preceded its Whyte number, so giving: 8P6F 4-6-2 (which was then further followed by the engine's specific number, and its particular name). A complete example would be: BR (British Railways) A4 Class (Streamlined 'Pacific') 8P6F 4-6-2 No 60007 'Sir Nigel Gresley'.

*Above: 'The Talisman', pulled by Gresley's streamlined A4 Pacific No 60025 'Falcon',
leaves King's Cross Station in London, on its first run to Edinburgh in September 1956.*

Crew and Maintenance

It should be remembered that the railways throughout Britain were a huge source of employment for many years, and had a massive infrastructure not only of physical systems, but also of workers, each with a very special duty, whether based at stations, in signal-boxes, in goods yards, in engine sheds or track side (including platelayers and gangers). As far as locomotives were concerned, at least two crew members were required to operate most engines. There would be a driver who had ultimate responsibility for the locomotive and its crew, and a fireman who was responsible for its performance. The engine driver (or engineer) started and stopped the locomotive, and controlled its speed, while the fireman maintained the fire, regulated steam pressure, and kept an eye on water levels. The driver and fireman generally worked in a cab at the boiler's "backhead". Bringing a large locomotive "into steam" could, in fact, take many hours of preparation, and once underway, the crew had to work closely as a team. Besides controlling the engine, the driver needed to be familiar with the route and terrain, anticipating gradients, curves, junctions and any potential hazards, while also knowing the position of signals and other markers. Indeed, a whole "language" of railway signs and signals was developed in order to allow adequate preparation for upcoming railway "events".

Main: A fireman stoking a steam engine's furnace while its driver looks ahead.

Above: Satirical colored etching by Henry Hughes illustrating the dramatic effects of a boiler exploding during a railway journey. In the early days of the railways this was a relatively frequent occurrence.

The minimum duties necessary after a locomotive had been run were cleaning, inspecting and oiling, including disposal of the coal fire. In preparing to move "off shed" and back into service, coal had to be replenished in the "supply bin" (or "bunker"), and water tanks refilled, and any parts of the locomotive that were worn had to be replaced. Boilers had "manholes" on top to allow for inspection and cleaning, and at the front was a smoke box door (which looked somewhat like a submarine hatch). Boilers and their components could suffer from various problems such as scale, sediment and corrosion, which impaired the performance of the engine, and it was important to keep water out of the cylinders when working, and only use "dry steam" (because "wet" or "saturated" steam contains suspended water droplets, which eventually damaged the cylinders). Boilers might also be damaged, or even fail and explode, if over-pressurised, or if they were poorly or crudely constructed – as many early boilers were, at least by modern standards. They might also overheat if they lacked sufficient water.

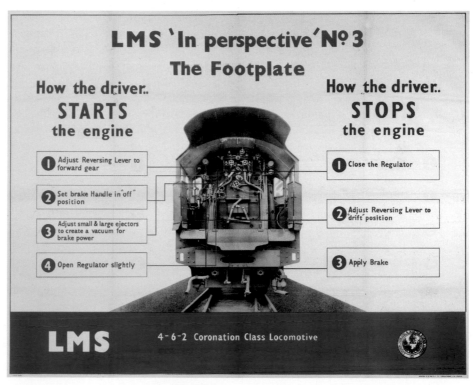

Above: Poster produced for the London, Midland & Scottish Railway advertising how a driver starts and stops an engine.

Just one of the reasons why very early locomotives were unsafe by modern standards is because they often had no brakes, and so needed to judge carefully when to start slowing, so as not to miss an approaching station. (Although very old and small locomotives did have a type of hand brake, which was initiated by a screw thread.) Most early locomotives relied on their valve gear to put the wheels into reverse if there was a real emergency. Later, "steam brakes" were developed (or steam-driven vacuum brakes – and indeed also air brakes), where – by means of a piston – a shoe or "brake block" was pressed onto a drive wheel, in order to help slow it. Even large locomotives ultimately had handbrakes as well (though these were mainly used for

securing the engine, once it was stationary in a shed or at a station). Brake blocks naturally needed regular checking and replacing due to the huge loads acting upon them. Likewise, the first locomotives, as well as their goods wagons and carriages, had few or only very basic "springs" – making for a very rough ride. They initially took their cue from the springs on horse-drawn carriages, which evolved into locomotive "leaf springs", attached to the chassis or mainframe of the locomotive by "spring hanger links". The axle box then came to contain "horn guides", between which slid up and down a sort of piston, fixed to the centre of the leaf spring, so that the wheels could overcome track irregularities, and not lose traction or grip.

Cylinders needed to be lubricated with a special type of steam cylinder oil, formulated in such a way that the oil did not emulsify at the very high temperatures and pressures at which steam cylinders operate. Grease or conventional bearing oil was used for the larger bearings. Thin oil was also used for slides and other bearings. Cylinder oil was usually pumped in mechanically, while above the bearings often sat little pots, or reservoirs, from which the required oil was then drip-fed by capillary action into the bearing via a wick or "trimming", made from wool ("trimmings of worsted yarn") – usually wound round with metal wire. In the 19th and 20th Centuries, there used to be much work for "oiler/greasers" in maintenance sheds, since even on fairly simple locomotives there could be upwards of 50 places that regularly needed oiling.

Above: A group of schoolboys are given a demonstration of engine-driving by a professional in April 1933.

Renewal

While steam locomotives may not be as plentiful or occupy as central a position as once they did in relation to transportation, it should be remembered that steam turbines are still very much in evidence throughout the world. Certainly, just as with steam locomotives, industrial uses of reciprocating steam engines declined as the 20th Century wore on – in the latter case thanks to the convenience of electricity that could be obtained down the end of a wire. But, in fact, steam did not die out at all – it was merely transformed, and then used in conjunction with other power sources – for steam turbines across the globe provide us to this day with the overwhelming proportion of our electricity needs.

Above: Could steam power come full circle? This steam-driven 1925 Doble Steamer Coupe was an early alternative fuel vehicle. It got about eight miles a gallon from just about anything that can be burned in a furnace, including reclaimed crankcase oil.

Steam turbines, steam engines and steam heating systems can have, as their sources of heat, a variety of fuels, some fossil-based and others relying on nuclear, solar or even geothermal energy. As ultra-clean and sustainable fuel sources are developed and encouraged in the future, it is not beyond the realms of possibility that steam may yet see a return to vehicle use in some manner: in automobiles perhaps, or even, once more, in a new generation of "clean" railway locomotives.

Left: Steam travel is still popular in the 21st Century with Heritage Railways thriving.

The Big Four

The 120 smaller railway companies were mostly amalgamated and grouped into the "Big Four" on 1 January 1923. These comprised the Great Western Railway (GWR), the London & North Eastern Railway (LNER), the London, Midland & Scottish Railway (LMS) and Southern Railway (SR). This grouping, formed as a result of the Railways Act 1921 - which came into effect in January 1923 - brought about the four largest railway companies in Britain. The term "Big Four" was coined by "Railway Magazine" in February 1923 when describing the new railway era, which was to last until the end of 1947.

The consolidation affected most of the railways in the country, however, a small number – which were already operating as joint railways – remained separate, including the Somerset & Dorset Joint Railway and the Midland & Great Northern Joint Railway. Some of the London suburban railway was also excluded from the act including the Metropolitan Railway and the light railways, which were already authorised under the Light Railways Act of 1896. The Act, under the government of Lloyd George, was brought in to prevent the financial losses experienced by the railways during the latter part of the 19th Century and into the 20th Century, mainly due to over-competition between local, rival companies.

*Above: Junction of the Midland, Great Northern and Metropolitan
railways at King's Cross, London, in January 1868.*

*Main: Claughton class 4-6-0 locomotive No 1914 'Patriot' was built in memory of London &
North Western employees who were killed in the First World War and was painted plain black. The
railway companies wanted to remember their workers who had been killed or injured in action.*

The British Government had taken control of the railways
during the First World War (1914-18), to enhance the war
effort, at a time when all businesses across the country
needed to work strategically together in order to gain
victory and beat the Axis powers. This status remained
into 1921 when the Act consolidating the railways was
introduced. The idea behind the legislation, as well
as stemming further financial losses, was to retain the
benefits that the railways had experienced under state
control. It had been mooted whether the railways should
be nationalized in the early part of the 1920s, but it was

rejected and nationalization didn't take place until nearly three years after the Second World War (1939-45) in January 1948. What the Act intended was an efficient reorganization of the railway companies which would, in turn, improve the economics of the industry.

By 1920, the Ministry of Transport had been in existence for nearly 12 months and was being pressed on all sides for a statement of policy. It was widely recognized that a return to pre-war competition was not in the best interests of the industry or the country. A unified railway system was deemed the best possible option and while the grouping was considered highly complex, operationally, it was initiated fairly quickly. As far back as 1911, through the Departmental Committee on Railway Agreements and Amalgamations, it was agreed that the merits of amalgamation brought about the development "of an improved and more economical railway system", and that a more "perfect cooperation between the railway companies" would lead to overall growth.

Above: A proposed freight transfer depot on the Great Western Railway, 1830s.

The Great Western Railway was founded in 1833 and quickly established itself as "God's Wonderful Railway", connecting the South West of England, particularly from Cornwall across the River Tamar, with the rest of the United Kingdom. However, this impressive feat in civil engineering wasn't always that direct in its approach to the rest of the West Country, Wales and London, and many dubbed it the "Great Way Round". It would become synonymous with the holiday railway, despite some of its early lines being somewhat disorganised, and GWR ferried literally millions of people from their homes across the British mainland to the seaside resorts around the Devon and Cornwall coastlines.

It was built mainly to service the great port of Bristol with its burgeoning businesses and direct links to the United States. The River Avon gave the city a unique position amongst Britain's cities, despite rising competition from other ports including Liverpool. It was the country's link for imports and exports, but the riverbed was quickly becoming clogged with silt. Over time, this situation made it increasingly difficult for Bristol to operate as an effective port but, while the railway infrastructure was still underway further west, it was an important dock for the trade route across the Atlantic.

The Great Western Railway was incorporated by an Act of Parliament in 1835. Isambard Kingdom Brunel (9 April 1806 – 15 September 1859) was appointed as chief engineer and was responsible for the pioneering bridge crossing from Saltash on the Cornish side of the River Tamar to the Devon side in Plymouth. This extraordinary structure is still in operation today, although heavy modern trains are faced with speed restrictions as they cross high above the river. Brunel carefully surveyed the route between Bristol and London himself, which minimized the gradients and curves on the line. He was the first engineer to pioneer the broad gauge line (as opposed to standard gauge), which provided two problems. The first concerned the cost of the project – while broad gauge provided more comfort for passengers, the engineering work was far more costly – and second, by not using standard gauge the engineer caused more "headaches" for the workforce when they needed to interconnect the lines with standard gauge. Another surprising decision by Brunel was to route the line through the Marlborough Downs, therefore bypassing major towns and cities. It would result in a spectacular line, which he devised with GWR's superintendent of locomotives, Daniel Gooch.

Opposite: GWR broad gauge locomotive 'Balaklava' in 1892. Note the narrower gauge rails within the broad gauge rails.

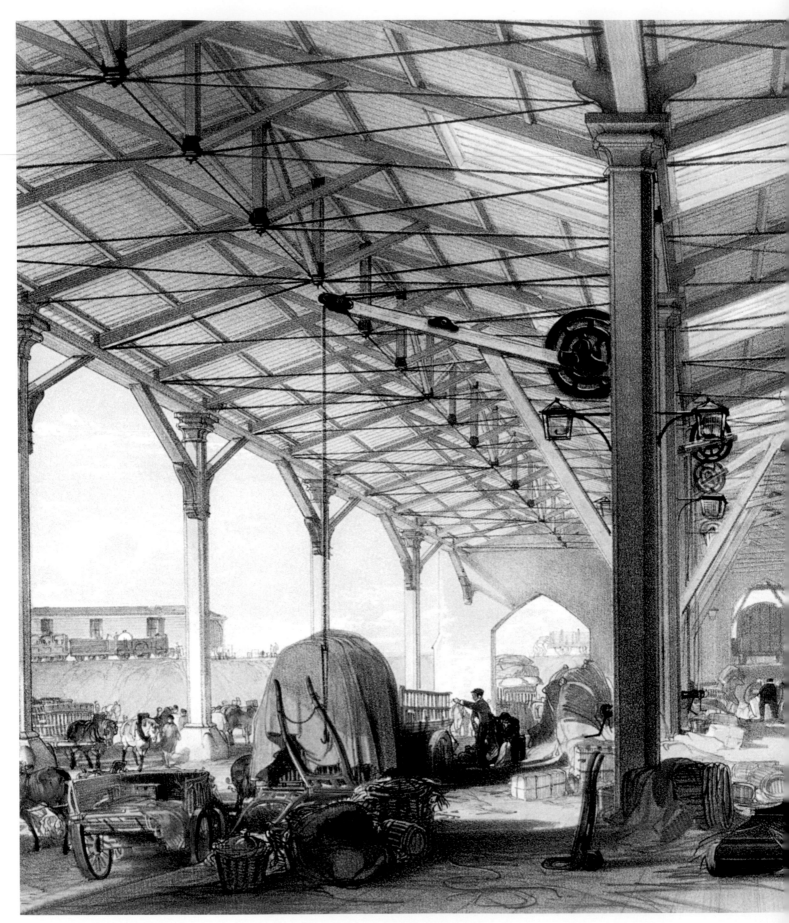

Main: A Great Western Railway freight shed at Bristol.

Above: The original masonry and timber structure of the Liskeard Viaduct carried the Cornwall Railway across a deep valley shortly before it entered Liskeard Station.

Above: An exterior view of Bristol Temple Meads.

Above: GWR abandoned the broad gauge system in 1892 and several miles of sidings were laid at Swindon. 130 of the 195 locomotives taken out of service were convertible and re-entered service as standard gauge engines.

The first stretch of the new line opened three years later and ran between London and Taplow. Six years after the line came under construction, locomotives could travel from London to Bristol Temple Meads following the completion of Box Tunnel (opened in 1841). Dug through Box Hill, between Bath and Chippenham, it was one of the most impressive structures on the GWR line at nearly two-miles long. (By 2016, Box Tunnel will be electrified as part of an electrified service to Bristol Temple Meads station.) However, its construction was considered impossible when the concept was discussed as early as 1835, although its make up of limestone, Lias Clay and Fuller's Earth (with high magnesium oxide content) would prove sceptics wrong. Brunel carefully assessed the strata the following year by sinking eight shafts at intervals through the hill and contractor George Burge was appointed as the tunnel's major player operating from the west, while local firm Lewis and Brewer worked on the construction from the east. While the terrain was certainly capable of being tunnelled, it

was a dangerous job for the navvies and around 100 lives were lost during construction. This led to inevitable delays and eventually the 1,200-strong workforce was increased to 4,000. Despite the hazardous nature of the job, Brunel's calculations were so precise that when the construction work from the east met those working from the west, there was less than two inches difference in their alignment.

Once the line was open, it was the locomotives that were to prove troublesome. They were unreliable and Daniel Gooch had to intervene to ensure that the journey from London to Bristol would become a resounding success. Swindon workshops became the centre for the locomotives that ran on the line. Over the following 20 or so years, lines were built, amalgamated and incorporated to include routes to Oxford, via the Oxford & Rugby Railway and the South Wales Railway, the Cornwall Railway, West Cornwall Railway and the South Devon Railway.

Before the Railway Regulation (Gauge) Act 1846 that dictated that all lines become standard gauge, Brunel's broad gauge lines required passengers travelling on the Birmingham & Gloucester Railway to change at Gloucester in order to travel on GWR. However, despite the 1846 Act, GWR were confident of their broad gauge lines and commissioned the world's first telegraph line running from London to West Drayton. They beat off rivals to build a line directly to Birmingham in 1852 and later extended this with broad gauge tracks to Wolverhampton. They did, however, concede to a standard gauge line to Birkenhead, and things further improved when the Midland Railway innovatively employed a third track so that standard or broad gauge locomotives and carriages could run on the lines when they acquired the Bristol & Gloucester Railway.

Above: The Royal Albert Bridge under construction over
the River Tamar at Saltash, Cornwall.

*Above: The 930 foot long Royal Albert Bridge
was built between 1854 and 1859.*

GWR and Midland Railway merged in 1861 and standard gauge lines became the mainstay of the railway network. It was at this point that lines were extended towards the South Devon coast and across the Tamar into Cornwall. The Royal Albert Bridge, so named for Queen Victoria's husband, enabled the railway line to reach as far west as Penzance (close to where Richard Trevithick's innovations in steam first took shape) in 1867. The bowstring suspension bridge was, and still is, an impressive sight across the Tamar and was Brunel's cleverly constructed answer to a problem. Comprising an iron arch, or "bow", the bridge is hung by huge suspension chains on each side of the tube. The line was then laid on a plate girder road. Even in the 21st Century the Royal Albert Bridge is a masterpiece in engineering and it remains unique as the only one in existence to carry mainline trains. Brunel then turned his attentions to another beautiful part of the country when he created the Wye Bridge, linking the South Wales Railway to Gloucestershire in 1852.

By 1873, GWR were ready to expand again, this time via a tunnel under the River Severn. It would allow a more direct route from the West Country to South Wales, but construction proved difficult and costly. The River Severn, while impressive in its course, delayed the building of the tunnel, which remained incomplete until 1886 when it opened. The network welcomed new locomotives including the Star Class and the Saint Class alongside the 2800 Class from the end of the 19th Century. GWR had almost 4,000 miles of railway lines by the time it was nationalized to form part of British Railways (which later became British Rail) on 1 January 1948.

The second line to form part of the "Big Four" was the London & North Eastern Railway (LNER), which was the second largest company brought about by the 1921 Railways Act. Sir Ralph Wedgwood (1874-1956) headed the company as chief general manager for the first 16 years of the amalgamation, responsible for a network of nearly 7,000 miles. He was an astute, pioneering businessman and a member of the Wedgwood family, (his great-great grandfather was Josiah Wedgwood) and he had a deep affection for steam locomotives. His immense interest in steam and its development had led him to North Eastern Railway in his early career. In 1902, he was made a district superintendent and in 1904 became secretary where he successfully established himself within the company. His passion for all things steam made him a great advocate of the "heart-beat" of Britain and his many roles (including a stint as a passenger manager) stood him in good stead when he became boss in 1923, having been promoted to general manager the year before. He ensured, through the empowerment and inspiration of his staff, that LNER was a successful company and he understood that from the boss to those working on the "front line" that each and every individual working on the railways was an essential component of a well-oiled machine – literally. He had worked his way up through the ranks and he never took his later status for granted, or forgot the hands-on experience he had gained as a young railway employee. Such was his reputation that he was asked by the government to manage the railway networks as Chair of the Railway Executive Committee for the duration of the Second World War.

*Above: A London & North Eastern Railway train hauling
a batch of ten new steamrollers from the Marshall and Sons
works in Lincolnshire in October 1925 destined for Greece.*

Above: Glenfinnan Viaduct (circa 1910) on the North British Railway
West Highland Extension represents the first use of concrete in the
building of a major railway structure.

LNER was relatively free of the infighting that seemed to dog other companies within the Grouping and the amalgamation of Great Eastern Railway, the Great Northern Railway, the Great North of Scotland Railway, the Great Central Railway, the North British Railway, the North Eastern Railway and the Hull & Barnsley Railway was a slick operation under Sir Ralph. These companies brought into the second largest grouping consisted of former consolidations between the likes of Great Eastern Railway (GER), which was formed in 1862 with the amalgamation of Eastern Counties Railway, the Norfolk Railway, the Eastern Union Railway, the Harwich Railway, Newmarket Railway, the East Anglian Light Railway and the East Suffolk Railway. Great Central Railway, which ran from Manchester to Sheffield, Grimsby and Cleethorpes and Barnsley, Scunthorpe and Doncaster to Grimsby was matched by the North of Scotland Railway. Here the network ran from the north east of Scotland serving the agricultural region between Aberdeen and Elgin.

The Great Northern Railway (GNR) eventually became the Great North Eastern Railway (GNER) when it branched out along the East Coast mainline and served London from King's Cross to the East Midlands, through Peterborough, Grantham and York. There were also branch lines to Sheffield and Wakefield as well as Boston. North British Railway (NBR) was responsible for operations between Edinburgh, Glasgow, Carlisle, Newcastle and Aberdeen. LNER was also responsible for four of London's stations including Fenchurch Street, which had belonged to the London & Blackwell Railway, King's Cross (previously owned by Great Northern Railway), Marylebone – a former asset of Great Central Railway – and Liverpool Street, formerly owned by Great Eastern Railway. The company also ran and maintained suburban services to Broad Street and Moorgate in the City of London.

Left: Dairymen transporting dairy products from the Wensleydale Pure Milk Society
bottling plant in Northallerton (next to the NER line) to the stations in Wensleydale,
April 1927, using the 'Cream Special'.

Above: The London & North Eastern Railway was the only company to have cinema coaches. Launched in 1935, they were used in conjunction with Pathe films.

Above: The coat of arms of the Midland & Great Northern Joint Railway.

LNER owned around 7,650 locomotives, more than 29,000 freight vehicles and 20,000 coaches at its height. It was a huge company responsible for a large portion of the rail network as well as steamers, riverboats, hotels, docks and harbours. The company was also co-owner of the Midland & Great Northern Joint Railway – the UK's largest joint railway – together with London, Midland & Scottish Railway (LMS). In 1936, just 12 years before nationalization, LNER took sole responsibility for the former joint venture. Main routes included the East Coast mainline from London to Edinburgh, together with routes from Edinburgh to Aberdeen and Inverness to the far Northwest. East Anglia was a further region under the company's remit and the main workshops were housed in Doncaster, supported by other, smaller workshops around the region.

Above: Women armed with brooms prepare to clean an LNER turntable during World War II in April 1942.

Sir Ralph and his thousands of staff were aided by the highly acclaimed mechanical engineer Sir Nigel Gresley (1876-1941), who was a personal friend. It was Gresley that would design some of the most famous locomotives in history including LNER Class A3 and LNER Class A4 (which boast the 'Flying Scotsman' and 'Mallard' respectively). Designed and built for speed, these engines would have an impressive and unprecedented history that still excites interest and passion in the 21st Century. The 'Flying Scotsman' was officially recorded as the first train to reach a speed of more than 100 mph – although the 'City of Truro' has a claim to be the "true" first 100 mph train – while 'Mallard' was officially recorded as the fastest train when it reached a staggering 126 mph. The Gresley conjugated valve gear was engineering at its best and produced high speeds which, in turn, brought down running costs. Edward Thompson joined LNER for a short time, where he was renowned for his freight and mixed-traffic locomotives. However, his relationship with Sir Nigel did not flourish and he soon parted company with LNER. Arthur Peppercorn joined the company in 1945 and was responsible for the A1 and A2 Pacific designs – the express passenger locomotives. Unlike Thompson, he was an admirer of Gresley and was influenced by the long-standing mechanical engineer's designs. His own locomotives were highly revered for their reliability. Like its contemporaries, LNER had little choice but to face nationalization at the beginning of 1948.

Above: Arthur Peppercorn.

*Above: Railway workers painting a locomotive at Doncaster Works
in November 1947, one of the last London & North Eastern Railway
locomotives to be manufactured before the railways were nationalized.*

Another of the "Big Four" was the London, Midland & Scottish Railway, (LMS) which was formed by the amalgamation of the Caledonian Railway, Furness Railway, the Glasgow & South Western Railway, the London & North Western Railway, the Highland Railway, Midland Railway and the North Staffordshire Railway. The company also inherited a number of subsidiary railways, which were kept under the LMS umbrella or leased to other companies. The company's main routes stretched along the West Coast and the mainline across the West Midlands as well as North West Scotland and London. The company was instrumental in the transportation of freight between Britain's major industrial centres. Unlike LNER, which suffered little trouble, LMS was dogged by infighting and disputes. So, despite being the largest transport organization in the world and the largest commercial business in Britain (as well as the country's second largest employer), it wasn't destined for great things and its financial results would prove disappointing.

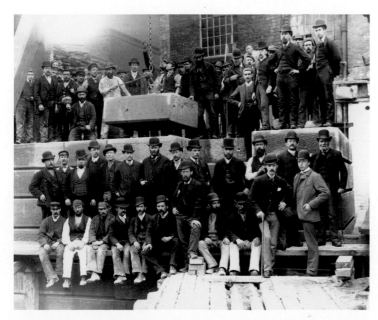

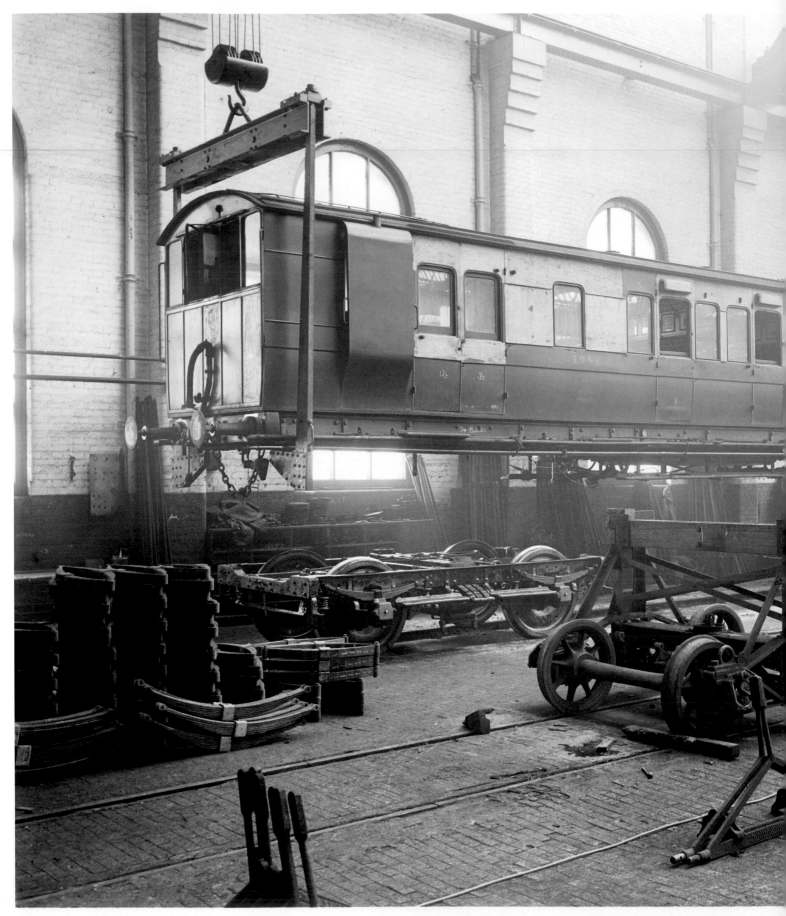

Above: Newton Heath carriage and wagon works in Greater Manchester closed in 1932, despite having one of the largest rolling stock outputs in Britain.

It was the only one of the "Big Four" to have operations across England, Scotland, Wales and Northern Ireland, but even this didn't ensure its financial success. The number of joint lines and its proximity to other railway companies – and therefore increased competition – despite its large geographical region, saw a rather haphazard company with a complicated infrastructure take shape. Most of the joint railways were on, or near, the boundaries with two or more of the Groups, which it could be argued placed LMS in a difficult position operationally. Together with LNER it ran the Midland & Great Northern Joint Railway and had another joint railway with Southern Railway (SR) in the guise of the Somerset & Dorset Joint Railway.

Above: London, Midland & Scottish Railway office at 43 New Oxford Street where passengers went to book and purchase their tickets.

*Above: Poster at Manchester's Victoria Station in March 1928 advertising
cheap tickets to holiday destinations over the Easter period.*

The network with SR caused further problems when
it ran through GWR's territory because it connected
Bournemouth and Bath. The company was operating with
a fairly substantial disadvantage from the start. Although
LMS was the largest and most central of the Groupings,
its numerous shared regions and boundaries meant stiff
competition from the likes of LNER for London-Scotland
routes, which mainly came down to passenger comfort and
the speed that journeys could be undertaken. Routes to the
East Midlands and Manchester were also hotly contested,
but the biggest competition came with GWR for passengers
travelling from London to Birmingham.

Coupled with the company's reputation for internal
disputes and disruptions, Chairman Josiah Stamp (1880-
1941) brought in mechanical engineer William Stanier
(1876-1965) in 1933. Stamp had a brilliant career in the
civil service – having left school at the age of 16 – and
rose to become a Director of the Bank of England. He
was a shrewd businessman and widely regarded as the
most knowledgeable man in the country when it came
to taxes. (So, it's perhaps surprising that the company
didn't perform more successfully financially.) He was a
sharp economist and became LMS's first president in
1926, although the railways were not to provide his finest
"hour" professionally and he failed to grasp that the
railway depended on its staff and their commitment to the

Below: Sir Josiah Charles Stamp (1880-1941), English economist and chairman of the London, Midland & Scottish Railway.

industry. He wrongly believed that the huge company under his control did not rely on the dedication and morale of the staff in his care. He turned things around somewhat with the appointment of Stanier who – like Sir Ralph Wedgwood at LNER – was passionate about the railways. Stanier had followed his father into a railway career, first with GWR in Swindon where he worked as a draughts man, before being promoted in 1900 to Inspector of Materials. He was then employed by George Church ward, a highly influential engineer who gave him the role of Divisional Locomotive Superintendent. He returned to Swindon in 1912 as Assistant Works Manager before becoming Chief Mechanical Engineer in 1920. Stanier joined LMS at a time when Stamp realized he needed professional help.

Above: Entrance to the First and Third Class refreshment rooms at Barrow Station, Cumbria, 11 February 1930. At this time different class passengers had different facilities in stations.

Above: A woman receives information leaflets from a publicity van belonging to the London, Midland & Scottish Railway Company in Blackpool.

From 1933 onwards, Stanier was pivotal in the development of the company and sorted the troubles between workers from the former Midland Railway and those from the former North Western Railway by introducing new ideas which both sides could adapt to fit their working practices. Disputes were soon over and a more settled and hands-on approach to running the business and caring for the workforce saw huge improvements. He reversed the "small engine policy" which the company had inherited from Midland Railway – where marketing was key and smaller, lighter locomotives were the mainstay of the business. This was unlike other companies, where the designer and their teams and the locomotives were the all-important aspects of the business and where longer trains prevailed, pulled by larger, but comparatively slower locomotives. He was aided in his quest to turn things around by the support of Josiah Stamp, who had struggled to understand the management needed of his railway prior to Stanier's appointment.

Before being amalgamated into LMS, the Caledonian Railway was a major Scottish line with works located in Glasgow, which linked Edinburgh, Glasgow and Carlisle. When the line to Carlisle – linking Scotland to London – eventually opened, it cut travelling times by hours (although it was still an incredibly long journey). Lines also included Aberdeen, Perth, Sterling and Dundee. North Staffordshire Railway also came under LMS in the Grouping in 1923. In its early years – after incorporation in 1845 – the company ran the Trent and Mersey Canal and the Derby and Crewe Railway. It was also responsible for the building of a number of lines including from Macclesfield to Crewe. The railway between Dalry and Kilmarnock was taken over by the Glasgow & South Western Railway, formed in 1843. The company also became responsible for the Kilmarnock & Troon Railway, and many Scottish lines were amalgamated into the railway company before it became part of LMS.

Below: Steam locomotives being prepared, including Jubilee Class 4-6-0 No 5559 'British Columbia', Coronation Class 4-6-2s No 6224 'Princess Alexandra' and the 'Duchess of Buccleuch' at the LMS Camden Motive Power Shed, 1938.

The final company to join the "Big Four" was Southern Railway (SR) with its famous locomotives including the 'Golden Arrow' and the 'Brighton Belle'. Terrain meant that it didn't have as much competition with LMS as LNER, or GWR, and amalgamations to form SR included South Eastern Railway, London & South Western Railway, London, Chatham & Dover Railway and Brighton & South Coast Railway. Smaller lines were also "swallowed" by the company in the Grouping in 1923. Competition came in another form, however, with the development of roads. Following the First World War, the infrastructure of Britain's roads came under scrutiny and changes and improvements were fairly rapid. Buses and cars now rivalled the railway company and by the end of the 1920s, national bus companies were seriously undermining the former glory of travelling by train.

Pendleton and Manchester saw the benefits of the first omnibus service in 1824 – while stagecoach services had been in operation for a number of years already. However, the omnibus service required no booking and was designed so that passengers could join and leave the route wherever they wished. London acquired its first omnibuses in 1829, at a time when rail services were not permitted into the centre of the capital. Horse bus services then developed but it wasn't until the law changed in 1896 that steam buses joined horse transport on Britain's streets. Petrol buses arrived by the turn of the 20th Century. (Great Western Railway was one of the first companies to incorporate petrol buses in the early 1900s between Helston and The Lizard in Cornwall.)

Right: Two new King Arthur class 4-6-0 locomotives, being towed by an 0-6-0 locomotive No 103, manufactured in Glasgow, but used on the Southern Railway.

*Above: The Isle of Wight was a popular holiday
destination and passengers were served by this Terrier
class steam train at 'Newport' in 1925.*

Above: A 1927 poster produced for the Southern Railway to promote southern routes as gateways to the sun.

These vehicles began to flourish by the time of the First World War and when the atrocities ended, many ex-servicemen – who had learnt mechanics during their time in the army – began bus companies of their own. In places like Cornwall, where there was one major line in and out of the county, supported by a small number of branch lines, buses were the only alternative for many. The Road Traffic Act 1930 also helped develop this competition with the railways by bringing in regulations for bus services. In the South West, Devon found its railways hard hit by the formation of the Western National Omnibus Company in 1929. It was the beginning of the end for many of the smaller branch lines.

Prior to the increased competition from bus companies, Southern Railway inherited a number of duplicate routes as a result of amalgamation. The London & South Western Railway (LSWR) came complete with management structures that held the most influence over the newly created grouping in 1923. Channel ports – and services to them – became a priority, while other lines were given less status. A management team was set up in the former LSWR offices in Waterloo, London, to oversee the newly inherited port and harbour facilities. These included Plymouth, Portsmouth, Southampton, Dover, Folkestone and Newhaven. It was serving the suburbs of London and surrounding areas, coupled with the fact that SR dealt in holiday passengers that would determine its status as a predominantly passenger-service company. It wasn't always a slick operation – with some infighting due to amalgamation – and there were various "headaches" to deal with.

Above: The Southern Railway engine 'Channel Packet' – one of the new Merchant Navy class of engines – on a trial run in March 1941, driven by Transport Minister John Moore-Brabazon.

Above: Under the instruction of the General Manager, the staff of a main London station of the Southern Railway, worked in their gas masks at regular periods during the Second World War.

Southern Railway's locomotive 'Lord Hood' was forced to use GWR lines to reach Plymouth when it was banned from using the railway's own lines. However, led by Sir Herbert Walker (1868-1949) and supported by mechanical engineers Richard Maunsell and later Oliver Bulleid, the company was well run and noted for its PR campaigns and efficient management. It was the smallest of the "Big Four" but the fact it had more passengers than freight, led to some noteworthy achievements. This included its operations during the Second World War – particularly its part in transporting troops during Dunkirk operations and its activities in 1944 as part of the logistics chain for Operation Overlord. Under Government control, in 1940, a munitions siding was constructed around Plymouth and many of the smaller, previously abandoned stations found themselves operational once again. Plymouth was particularly at risk during the Second World War and the Southern Railway became instrumental in the war effort. As the company had roughly 75 per cent passenger traffic prior to the war, when the railway was required to lend its services to the Allied troops, a worrying shortage of freight locomotives was solved by Chief Mechanical Engineer Bulleid, and the volume of traffic was satisfied. The railway territory was also positioned right on the South Coast where it was believed enemy troops would land should they manage to invade Britain.

Above: Holiday crowds at Waterloo Station, London, 1946.

Above: The novel and controversial design of the Bulleid "tavern" car originated on the Southern Railway before nationalization.

Southern Railway inherited around 24 and a half miles of electrified railway in 1923 in overhead line and electrified lines that totalled around 59 miles (including a short stretch on the Waterloo & City Railway – underground). This was increased two years later to include routes to Surrey, including cities like Guildford, and areas of Kent by the use of a third rail and, by 1926, electric trains were running on the South Eastern mainline. The third rail provided 660V DC and eventually replaced the previous AC system in 1929. Many plans to electrify the lines across the South East were delayed by the Second World War by up to 20 years. However, much of the modernisation carried out by Southern Railway prior to the Wall Street Crash in 1929 and the economic crisis of the 1930s saw the company fare better than most as it maintained its financial position during the Depression.

The company, alongside GWR, was responsible for the "holiday" trains which reached the South and South West coasts. With steep gradients in places along the Mendip Hills (requiring double heading in places – the use of two locomotives) on the mainline, the lines ran from Bath to Bournemouth West, with branch lines to Burnham-on-Sea, Wells and Bridgwater.

Above: Southern Railway West Country class 4-6-2 steam locomotive No 21C110 'Sidmouth', newly completed at Eastleigh Works, 1945.

The Fall of Steam Railways

On 1 January 1948, the "Big Four" were nationalized to form British Railways and found themselves under the control of the British Transport Commission. Initial changes were few and continued use of services maintained a profitable network, to some degree.

However, between the start of nationalization and 1954, the railways underwent a number of regeneration schemes – to tracks and stations – but that same year also saw the privatization of road haulage following structural changes at the British Transport Commission. Transport across Britain was no longer coordinated and the panic-introduction of diesel and electric rolling stock as part of British Railways modernisation plans saw profits plummeting to an all-time low.

Right: A sign painter obliterates the familiar Great Western Railway logo in January 1948 with the nationalization of the railways.

Above: Young visitors queue up to stand on the footplate of a new Battle of Britain Class locomotive, the 'Sir Eustace Missenden', during an open day at a locomotive works in Ashford, 31 August 1949.

Above: An overhead hopper fills the tender of a British Railways steam engine with coal in 1948.

These new trains were seen as the future – they were developed and championed, and steam locomotives with their older technology were deemed "unfit" for service. This was mainly because they needed constant maintenance, often with fairly basic working tools, while the "simple" working parts demanded a great deal of attention. Labour was extremely intensive, and locomotives required enormous amounts of fuel and water for what became seen as an inefficient mode of transport. The rise of the motorcar did not help the cause, with many influential politicians and business leaders becoming pivotal in the development of road networks. Steam was, by now, considered outdated and new technologies were seen as the only way forward for many of the network's services. However, the millions of pounds that this investment required would never be recouped. Some networks across the globe did manage to hang on to their steam locomotives until the latter part of 20th Century, but these were few and far between. New horizons were envisaged, and the age of steam was effectively over.

In Britain, losses mounted and cutbacks were inevitable. A major reduction in the network was planned, and the government asked Dr Richard Beeching to reorganize the railways. Commonly known as "The Beeching Axe", the resulting policy led to a major decline in Britain's railways. Many branch lines were closed for economic reasons and a large number of rural services lost their stations for good, which in turn saw feeder lines with reduced passenger numbers putting mainline stations and services at a further disadvantage. Freight services began transferring to road haulage and, while the public were less than supportive of the measures, the government and Dr Beeching remained determined. Steam locomotives that had once brought the British countryside to life, and had transformed the modern world with an infrastructure that wowed the rest of the globe, were to grace the rail network no longer.

Above: 'Hornet's Beauty' A2 Class steam locomotive at Leeds Central station, circa 1954, while a diesel train leaves for Castleford.

Methods of Traction

ELECTRIC YEAR 1956

No. of Locomotives	71
No. of Motor Passenger Coaches	2,262
Electricity used for traction (units)	964,525,000

STEAM YEAR 1956

No. of Locomotives	17,522
Total Weight (tons)	1,231,638
Average per loco. (tons)	70·29
Coal used (miles per ton)	37·36

DIESEL YEAR 1956

No. of Locomotives	609
Diesel Train vehicles motor and trailer	455

YEAR	TOTAL OF LOCOMOTIVES (No.)	MILES RUN (thousands)	NET TON MILES (Tonnage x distance carried) (millions)	PASSENGER MILES (No. of passengers x distance carried) (millions)
1938	19,644	584,461	16,672	19,702
1948	20,302	537,460	21,662	21,022
1952	19,133	538,252	22,391	20,459
1954	18,816	535,649	22,089	20,712
1956	18,207	527,635	21,473	21,133

THE WORK DONE

THE FUTURE THE LAST EXPRESS PASSENGER AND SUBURBAN STEAM LOCOMOTIVES WERE BUILT IN 1956. DIESEL AND ELECTRIC TRACTION WILL GRADUALLY, BUT AT AN INCREASING PACE, SUPERSEDE STEAM FOR

QUICK CLEAN COMFORTABLE TRAVEL

BRITISH RAILWAYS

Left: Despite the encroachment of diesels on the railways, it was a steam train that was chosen to carry King George VI's coffin from Paddington Station, London, to Windsor in February 1952.

Above: It wasn't just the steam locomotives that were under threat of modernisation. This is the grand roof over the platforms of Cannon Street Station, London, in April 1958 just before it was dismantled.

With some economic recovery following the Second World War, the mid-1950s saw real investment in diesel locomotive technology and diesel began to dominate. Labour-intensive maintenance gave way to greater performance and flexibility but, most importantly, reduced operating costs. However, the future demise of steam began much earlier in 1896, with the forerunner of diesel, when Herbert Akroyd Stuart designed the world's first oil-engine locomotive for the Royal Arsenal at Woolwich. (This is widely regarded as not strictly being a diesel engine because of the use of a hot bulb engine [also referred to as a semi-diesel].) The first engines designed

Above: A British Railways poster from the 1950s aimed at encouraging people to travel by train.

Above: This 1950s poster shows illustrations of 21 examples of the company's locomotives, with information regarding each one detailed beneath the image.

under Diesel were unsuitable for propelling land-based locomotives (and other types of vehicles), although they worked well for stationary and marine-propelled machines. Continued experiments and prototypes led to a locomotive on the Winterthur-Romanshorn Railroad claiming its place in history as the world's first diesel-powered locomotive in 1912. While commercially unsuccessful, this "first" encouraged the production of other prototypes throughout the 1920s. By 1929, Denmark had built a locomotive with two bogies – a wheeled wagon – through the workshops of Burmeister and Wain.

By the 1960s, Britain, as well as other countries across Europe and the United States were on the cusp of a future with diesel locomotives. Throughout the 1960s and 1970s, diesel became widespread and, unlike steam, the changes were rapid but, in line with early steam locomotives, these diesel engines were prone to breakdowns. There was a slightly different story in Northern Ireland, where the rail network was allowed to wither. Efforts were made in the Republic to keep steam on track – and turf became the ultimate fuel due to a lack of coal – but eventually, diesel locomotives were employed when defeat was conceded.

*Above: Crowds turn out to say farewell to the last train from
Ruabon to Blaenau Ffestiniog, Wales, in January 1961.*

Meanwhile, in England, Scotland and Wales, branches lines – once an important part of the lifeblood of the British network – began to wane. The future looked bleak. This futile future was emphasized by the arrival of bus services, which often literally dropped passengers outside their own front doors. This competitive, rival transport had been steadily gaining in momentum for more than 40 years by the end of the 1960s. Until 1930, there had been no major legislative changes on road traffic since the Motor Car Act 1903. While some changes had been discussed in Parliament, it wasn't until 1929 that serious debate got underway, which led to the Road Traffic Act 1930.

This new legislation overrode not just the Motor Car Act 1903, but the Locomotive Act 1865 and the Locomotives on Highways Act 1896 and saw a number of new regulations firmly established. Most importantly, these included the first ever driving tests in Britain (for disabled drivers only), the introduction of driving offences, compulsory insurance (third-party only) and the classification of cars. For commercial vehicles, including buses, the new legislation brought in central regulation of services, the introduction of a 30 mile-an-hour speed limit, rules and regulations for the conduct of drivers, conductors and passengers, and a limit on the numbers of hours that a driver could operate the vehicle. With a more efficient and regulated industry forming, more direct routes and greater availability, locomotives found their previous dominance on the decline.

The Advanced Passenger Train, or APT was in place – in a counter move by British Railways – by 1973, which was enhanced two years later by the advent of the High Speed Train (HST). The railways, it seemed, were about to change their recent misfortunes. But, British Railways were about to be greatly undermined by one man – a man synonymous with the demise of steam and rail travel in general. That man was Dr Richard Beeching. While some regarded Beeching as a saviour of the railways, many more deemed that he destroyed them.

BRITAIN'S FIRST ALL-ELECTRIC

January 1955 saw the completion of electrification of the Manchester-Sheffield-Wath lines of British Railways to afford the first example, in this country, of a main line over which all passenger and freight train operation is carried out by electric traction.

The Manchester, Glossop and Hadfield suburban service is provided by multiple-unit electric trains, but elsewhere all haulage is performed by mixed traffic electric locomotives of the two types depicted in the above view of the line between Hadfield and Woodhead.

In the centre is a Manche
2,760 h.p. Co–Co (12 wheeled d
work. On the left is a westbo
eight 1,868 h.p. Bo+Bo (8 wheel

Over the Manchester-Sheffie
every 24 hours, nine out of ten

BRITISH RAILWAYS

Above: A poster produced for British Railways' London Midland Region (LMR)
in 1955, promoting the first mainline service in Britain to operate all freight
and passenger services by electric traction.

AIN LINE

ondon Road)—London (Marylebone) express headed by
bogie) locomotive No. 27000, of which seven are now at
al train hauled by No. 26051, one of a fleet of fifty-
ble bogie) locomotives in service.

line there are operated about 100 trains each way
ich consist of loaded coal wagons or empties

*Above: Dr Richard Beeching, left, pictured in London in discussion
with Ernest Marples, the Minister of Transport, in October 1962.*

*Above: Railway carriages are stored at Kingscote Station on
the disused Bluebell & Primrose Line between Lewes and
East Grinstead, in March 1959.*

It was the Labour Party's manifesto at the General Election in 1945 that promised to nationalize Britain's transport infrastructure. This would include everything except private vehicles (mainly cars), and the Transport Act 1947 came under the control of the British Transport Commission. The Act intended to create an integrated transport service – including the railways – but by 1951, the Conservative Party had little choice but to denationalize the road network.

Road transport – namely haulage companies – had been unable to compete with the transportation costs of the railways for a number of years. However, the formation of an executive committee, including Beeching, in 1960 would bring about radical change. The committee recommended the disbanding of the British Transport Commission. Beeching (1913-85) had joined the advisory group – whose aim was to look into the financial state of the Commission – chaired by Sir Ivan Stedeford when Sir Frank Smith (a scientist and chief engineer) recommended him. This was accepted by Conservative Minister of Transport, Ernest Marples, who knew that Sir Frank and Beeching had worked together at the Armament Design and Research Departments (within the Ministry of Supply during the Second World War).

Above: 'Caerphilly Castle' locomotive in transit to the Science Museum, London, 1963.

Sir Ivan, however, was unimpressed by Beeching's proposals to drastically reduce Britain's rail infrastructure and the two men clashed regularly on the aims and objectives of the advisory committee. Sir Ivan was invited to chair the advisory committee by then Prime Minister Harold Macmillan and the group became known as the Stedeford Committee. Sir Ivan wrote a report on the state of British transport which didn't gain any recognition for some time as it remained unpublished, despite questions being asked by Parliament. Instead, it was Beeching that provided a "plan" to reduce the railways.

In March 1961, Marples announced in the House of Commons that Beeching would become the first Chairman of British Railways in June that year. The Board would replace the British Transport Commission (which was disbanded in 1962 by the Transport Act). He was to come to prominence in a controversial position (with an equally controversial salary) earning more than the Prime Minister and his predecessor, Sir Brian Robertson, at the British Transport Commission. His staggering salary of £24,000 was more than two and a half times higher than that of any business leader in a nationalized environment at the time. He was seconded from his role at Imperial Chemical

Industries (ICI) – where he had also worked with Sir Frank Smith – for five years.

Beeching hailed from the Isle of Sheppey in Kent, the son of a journalist and teacher and the second of four brothers. After the family moved to Maidstone, Beeching attended a local school before moving to Maidstone Grammar School. Upon completing his schooling, Beeching enrolled at the Imperial College of Science & Technology where he read physics. He gained a First Class honours degree at his London college, where he remained to take his PhD. He worked in research between 1936 and 1943 before joining Mond Nickel Laboratories as a senior physicist. He married in 1938 and, during the Second World War, was sent on secondment to the Ministry of Supply at Fort Halstead. Following the war, he returned to ICI to take up the position of Technical Director, although he continued his work in armaments. He became an assistant to Sir Frank and was subsequently appointed to the ICI Fibres Division board. After two years in Canada working in other areas for the company he returned to Britain to take up the post of Chairman in the ICI Metals Division before being appointed to the ICI board as Technical Director.

Above: The past met the future in the 1980s when a replica of Stephenson's 'Rocket' ran alongside British Rail's modern Intercity train.

Right: 'Mallard' in the engine-shed at Nine Elms station, in south London, in February 1964. It is on its final journey from Doncaster (where it was built) to the Museum of British Transport in Clapham where it would go on permanent display.

Above: Dr Richard Beeching holding a copy of his plans for the reshaping of Britain's railways.

When Beeching joined the advisory committee, chaired by Sir Ivan in 1960, there was already widespread concern about Britain's transport industries. The railways had received substantial re-investment in the Modernisation Plan of 1955, yet still continued to suffer from huge losses. Passenger and freight traffic was in a steady decline and Beeching was tasked with turning the railways' fortunes around and ensuring that losses became profits. "The Reshaping of British Railways" was published on 27 March 1963. Beeching's recommendations would prove shocking.

He believed that British Railways should be run as a business, rather than a pure public service. He advocated that lines that could not support themselves should no longer be in operation. He suggested that savings of up to £147 million could be made by closing one-third of the country's railway stations – a total of around 2,400 – as well as scrapping around one third of freight services, and that some passenger services would need to be withdrawn. It was estimated that this would reduce around 5,000 route miles of services available, while more than 70,000 railway jobs (over a period of three years) would be lost. Trade Unions were horrified by the report. The Labour Party was outraged and the public were scathing of Beeching's recommendations.

Left: Pre and post Beeching map – the red on the map signifies those lines which were closed.

Beeching argued that cuts made economic sense in a failing industry and that in order to turn British Railways' fortunes around, there was little option. He was determined in his quest to scale back on operations and claimed he was facilitating necessary "surgery". Other measures that Beeching advocated included using block trains more regularly in his attempts to modernise the network. Block trains (or unit trains) comprised cars that all left one destination and ended up together in another. This was opposed to wagon load trains where costs proved greater due to the assembling and disassembling of trains en route, while delays were inevitable as carriages were split up or stored. Beeching advocated that block trains would provide a much more efficient and competitive environment, although it was widely regarded that they were only economical with high-volume traffic. After four years as Chairman of British Railways, Beeching returned to ICI in June 1965. He made an early return to his former position after compiling his second report with which the government did not agree.

This second Beeching report was published in February 1965 announcing a further stage of redevelopment and investment for 3,000 miles of trunk railway. Originally twice that mileage had been recommended. Under Beeching, the new recommendations allowed for the network to be routed through a number of selected lines including Scotland, Manchester, Liverpool, Coventry and Birmingham (all to be routed through the West Coast mainline), up to Carlisle and Glasgow. Northeast traffic was linked via the East Coast mainline while the Great Western mainline would cater for the West Country and Wales. Beeching strongly believed that the rail network comprised far too much duplication, but the government rejected his proposals. Whether he was sacked, or left by mutual agreement, is somewhat unclear although his policies were widely regarded as hard hitting, unnecessary and controversial. What is clear, however, is that whether consciously, or unconsciously, Beeching brought about a number of social consequences. His job had been to revolutionise Britain's railways. He had been tasked with turning a Victorian relic – with huge insurmountable losses – into a leading-edge network, which would see the country into the 21st Century; but many believed, and still do today (frustration and fury still runs high), that Beeching made a complete hash of the railways. Many commentators claimed that Beeching "butchered" the railways. His proposals eventually led to the closure of 5,500 miles of track, the shutdown of 2,363 stations and the loss of 67,000 jobs. His actions were further compounded when it was proved that the bus services that replaced the railways did not live up to expectations.

Right: Freight traffic handled in slow, loose-coupled unbraked vehicles in trains made up of single wagon loads proved vulnerable to road competition.

His further proposals were even more controversial with recommendations that another 4,500 miles should go, with links to Scotland, Wales and the West Country suffering virtual isolation. Despite all the controversy, and the intervention of the government who obviously did not believe Beeching was right, it was possible at the time to argue that the man from ICI had been correct in his findings and proposals. Over time, opinions changed and, today, with more people taking the train than ever before, it is acceptable to argue the opposite. A number of the routes that Beeching proposed should be "axed" managed to survive, thanks to well-fought opposition, and where once stations and routes were abandoned, today, including in the Welsh Valleys, services have been restored. These services are thriving and some lines are undergoing reinvestment in order to open them to passenger and freight traffic once more.

Beeching was accused of ignoring the economics that could, or might have, saved some lines, and that he was a naïve figure who "messed" up the financial figures. He was accused of being part of a conspiracy against the railways alongside government ministers, senior civil servants and others. He has even been called a scapegoat, where some have cited that ministers were wholly to blame for the massacre of Britain's railway network.

Beeching may have delivered a drastic and brutal blow through the publication of his report, but it was also a reaction to the significant losses suffered with the growth in private vehicles – one in nine families owned a car by the early 1960s – and cheaper bus fares. Beeching believed, as did many others, that the railways were a significant, if underachieving relic from a Victorian past. He advocated that while smaller lines and branch lines had long outlived their purpose, the main lines were still worth investment. He believed that the main lines, and the main lines only, could achieve the profits sought by the government. He was adamant that by closing the stations and branch lines he was shutting down a drain on resources – he did not believe, for example, that by doing so he was cutting off the heartbeat of the nation.

The closures had been taking place for almost a decade when Beeching published his report. He stepped up the pace, was brutal in his approach, and inflamed a situation that, in truth, was already being implemented. Before he left British Railways, there had been widespread speculation that Beeching would head the government's new board responsible for the infrastructure of the road and rail networks, but Minister of Transport Tom Fraser announced in the Commons that Beeching would leave his position as chairman in the summer of 1965.

In a statement, Fraser said: " … it is Dr Beeching's desire to return to ICI by the middle of next year … I have come to the conclusion that it would not be practicable for him to carry out the sort of study the government want … during the time." Beeching, it was cited at the time, preferred to work alone on his research and proposals, rather than working with other departments or the unions. Fifty years later and debate still goes on. While some see Beeching as a "mad axe man" who all but destroyed the railways, there are those who feel that he was a visionary who defied the unions to drag Britain out of the steam age. Whatever personal views commentators on Beeching may have, there is no doubting that he made an enormous impact, one way or the other. British Railways became British Rail in 1965 and the company was privatized between 1994 and 1997.

Right: The station at Chedworth in Gloucestershire was axed under the Beeching plan and by October 1964 was rapidly returning to nature.

By the end of the 1960s, Britain's scrap yards – particularly at Barry in South Wales – were full of aging locomotives, no longer fit to run on the rail network. Then something unexpected began to happen. Private investors and preservation societies began buying up the locomotives in order to restore them to their former glory. The first locomotive to be "rescued" in Barry was LMS 4F 0-6-0 (No 43924) in September 1968. By October that year, a number of locomotives were being moved to new homes. The preservation of steam locomotives began in earnest from this point on, although it decreased – in terms of sales of locomotives – from the end of the 1970s. Volunteers across the country worked together to save many locomotives and rolling stock from the breakers' yards, and finance came from a variety of sources. Preservation societies rely heavily on volunteers who are crucial to the survival of steam locomotives into the 21st Century. Thanks to these volunteers, steam travel is still possible and, for many, it remains a popular pastime.

SCAN WITH
layar
See page 5
for instructions

Above: Woodham's scrap yard was meant to have broken up over 200 locomotives that were withdrawn from British Railways' service at the end of steam in the 1960s, however nearly all of them were saved by preservation groups.

Above: Steam is still going strong in the 21st Century.

Index

Page numbers in *italics* indicate illustrations

Picture credits